Sacred Music Companion Fact Book

~

The chronological history
of our favorite traditional hymns & gospel songs
and the authors and composers who created them
By Dale V. Nobbman

Despite an exhaustive search, we have been unable to locate the publishers or copyright owners of some of the songs in this book. Therefore, we have proceeded on the assumption that no formal copyright claims have been filed on these works. If we have inadvertently published a previously copyrighted composition without permission, we advise the copyright owner(s) to contact us so that we may give credit in future editions.

ISBN 1-57424-112-5
SAB 683-8022

782.27
NOB

~Contents~

~Dedication~

This book is dedicated to all the writers and composers of our traditional hymns. Their songs have been a source of inspiration for generations of people around the world. John Greenleaf Whittier, America's beloved Quaker poet, once stated that "a good hymn is the best use to which poetry can be devoted".

~

Scripture from Psalm 104:33 states:

I will sing unto the Lord
As long as I live:
I will sing praise to my God
While I have my being.

~

The creation of our favorite traditional hymns and gospel songs began as a trickle up till the 1820's, at which time the number of songs began to stream from the pens of the authors and composers. The floodgates opened regarding the number of enduring songs published, beginning with the Civil War years, and that trend continues to the present.

~Foreword~

My criteria for selecting the featured 99 songs were first, they had to be song with "famous titles" that would be easily recognized by a majority of people. Secondly, I had to narrow the field of songs down to 99 by choosing the songs for which I could find a good deal of facts and interesting material to chronicle. The final selections were, I supposed, a bit subjective in that I picked "my" favorite songs that I grew up singing in our small-town Nebraska Methodist church. Our small village of Pleasant Dale was basically a farming community and I'm just old enough to have had the privilege of attending church, as a youth, with people born in the 19th century, and these are the songs I remember our little Midwest congregation of reverent and hardworking farm families singing.
Dale Nobbman

Doxology

Words by: Thomas Ken (1637-1711) in 1674
Composed by: Louis Bourgeois (c.1510-c.1561) in 1551
Original Title "Praise God From Whom All Blessings Flow"
Scripture Reference: Psalm 150:1

As a hymn of praise to God in Protestant churches since 1674, the lines of the "Doxology" are quite likely the most frequently sung words of any song in history. It perhaps has done more to teach the doctrine of the Trinity than all theology books put together. The words to this hymn were included in "Awake, My Soul, and With the Sun" by Ken in 1674, but it was not until 1694 that the "Doxology" became its own hymn.

Thomas Ken was born in Herfordshire, England, and lost his parents early in life. He was ordained in 1662 and became the Bishop of Bath and Wells in 1685. He was one of the most formidable churchmen of 17th century England and was known to have opposed declarations by both King Charles II and King James II, and refused to swear allegiance to William and Mary.

The musical setting for this hymn is from the "Genevan Psalter", first published in 1551 by Louis Bourgeois. Bourgeois was born in Paris, but moved to Geneva, Switzerland in 1541 and became an ardent follower of John Calvin. His tune name for this hymn is "Old Hundredth".

Historical Setting For **"DOXOLOGY"**

Spain was at the peak of its political and economic power in 1551.
The Dutch briefly reclaimed New Netherland from the English for a period of eight months in 1673.
The crop of rice was introduced to South Carolina in 1694.

Doxology

Words by THOMAS KEN
Music by LOUIS BOURGEIOS

Praise God, from whom all bless - ings flow; Praise

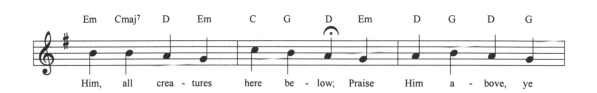

Him, all crea - tures here be - low; Praise Him a - bove, ye

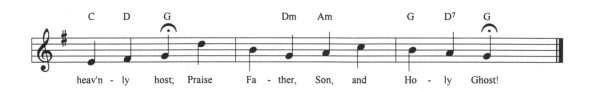

heav'n - ly host; Praise Fa - ther, Son, and Ho - ly Ghost!

O God, Our Help In Ages Past

Words by: Isaac Watts (1674-1748) in 1719
Composed by: William Croft (1678-1727) in 1708
Original Title: "Our God, Our Help In Ages Past"
Scripture Reference: Psalm 90

Isaac Watts is considered the "Father of English Hymnody". Watts was skilled at creating original compositions, and at adapting psalms in modern Christian language. He based this text on the 90th Psalm. The original hymn title was "Our God, Our Help In Ages Past". It was published in Watts' "The Psalms of David" in 1719. Watts published the first of his many hymn collections in 1707, and went on to write nearly 600 hymns, with this one perhaps being the best known.

William Croft was an English organist and choirmaster. Early in his life he composed music for the secular theater. Later he devoted himself completely to sacred music. He is considered one of the greatest English composers of church music and is credited with pioneering the writing of the English psalm tunes. The tune name for this hymn by Watts, the first prolific writer of hymns, is "St. Anne", named for the London church where Croft became organist in 1700. The tune was composed in 1708 and published that year in Tate & Brady's "Supplement to the New Version of Psalms".

Historical Setting For "O GOD, OUR HELP IN AGES PAST"

Johann Sebastian Bach became court organist at Weimar, Germany in 1708.
The American colony of Carolina consisted of 2,400 whites, 2,900 blacks slaves, and 1,100 Indian slaves in 1708.
Daniel Defoe published "Robinson Crusoe" in 1719.

O God, Our Help in Ages Past

Words by ISAAC WATTS
Music by WILLIAM CROFT

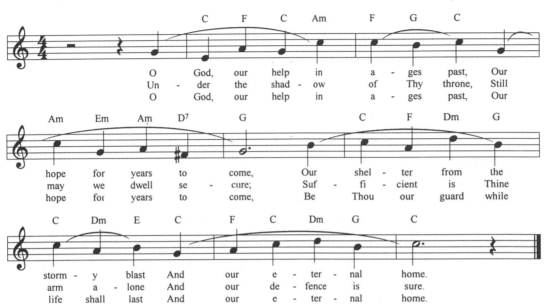

O God, our help in a - ges past, Our
Un - der the shad - ow of Thy throne, Still
O God, our help in a - ges past, Our

hope for years to come, Our shel - ter from the
may we dwell se - cure; Suf - fi - cient from is Thine
hope for years to come, Be Thou our guard while

storm - y blast And our e - ter - nal home.
arm a - lone And our de - fence is sure.
life shall last And our e - ter - nal home.

Christ The Lord Is Risen Today

Words by: Charles Wesley (1707-1788) in 1739
Tune from "Lyra Davidica" in 1708
Original Title: "Hymn For Easter"
Scripture Reference: I Corinthians 15:57 Matthew 28:5-6

Charles Wesley was born in Epworth, England. He became a prolific hymn writer, and co-founded Methodism with his brother, John Wesley. This hymn by Wesley was inspired by a 14th century Latin composition titled "Jesus Christ Is Risen To-Day". Wesley composed the hymn in 1739, one year after Wesley's conversion at Aldersgate, and was written for the first service held in the Foundry Meeting House chapel in London, England. It is the first of many popular hymns written by Wesley, and is one of the church's most popular Easter hymns.

The original hymn title was "Hymn for Easter" when it was published in Wesley's "Hymns and Sacred Poems" in 1739. The "Easter Hymn" tune was from an anonymous hymn collection titled "Lyra Davidica" in 1708. Revivalist, George Whitefield made changes to the text in 1753, and Martin Madan made some additional alterations in his "Psalms and Hymns" of 1760.

Speaking in regards to his works being altered, Wesley wrote a preface in one of his hymnals: "Many gentlemen have done my brother and me the honour to reprint many of our hymns. Now they are perfectly welcome to do so, provided they print them just as they are. But I desire they would not attempt to mend them, for they are really not able".

Historical Setting For "CHRIST THE LORD IS RISEN TODAY"

The United East India Company of Britain was created in 1708 and was the strongest European trading company on the coasts of India.
John Wesley began preaching in the fields at Bristol and buys a deserted gun factory outside London for his prayer meetings in 1739.
Scottish philosopher, David Hume, published his "Treatise on Human Nature" in 1739.

Christ the Lord is Risen Today

Words by CHARLES WESLEY

1. Christ the Lord is ris'n to - day,_____ Al - le -

lu - ia! Sons of men and an - gels say;_____

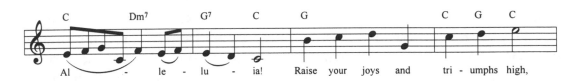

Al - le - lu - ia! Raise your joys and tri - umphs high,

Al - le - lu - ia! Sing___ ye___ heavn's and

earth re - ply,_____ Al - le - lu - ia!

2. Lives again our glorious King; Alleluia!
   Where, O death, is now thy sting? Alleluia!
   Dying once, He all doth save; Alleluia!
   Where thy victory, O grave? Alleluia!

3. Soar we now, where Christ has led, Alleluia!
   Foll'wing our exalted Head; Alleluia!
   Made like Him, like Him we rise; Alleluia!
   Ours the cross, the grave, the skies, Alleluia!

All Hail The Power Of Jesus' Name

Words by Edward Perronet (1726-1792) in 1780
4th Verse Words by: John Rippon (1751-1836) in 1787
Composed by Oliver Holden (1765-1844) in 1792
Original Title: "On the Resurrection, the Lord is King"
Scripture Reference: Revelation 19:16 Psalm 8:9 Phillippians 2:9-11

Ed Perronet was born in Sundridge, England, in 1726. He came from a distinguished French Huguenots family who had fled to Switzerland and then England to escape religious persecution. He was ordained an Anglican minister, and devoted much of his life to attacking abuses within the Church of England.

Perronet became a close friend of John and Charles Wesley. After a disagreement with the Wesley brothers, Perronet's hymns were banned from Methodist hymnals.

Oliver Holden, an American carpenter-composer, found that these lyrics fit his new tune "Coronation" perfectly, and the hymn became a favorite, especially among the Methodists. This hymn has sometimes been called the "National Anthem of Christendom". Perronet wrote this hymn text in 1780 and his original eight verses appeared in the "Gospel Magazine" that year. It was published again in "Occasional Verses, Moral and Sacred" in London in 1785.

John Rippon was one of the most influential ministers of his day. He published many of his sermons over a 63 year span of pastoring at a Baptist church in London, and edited several hymnbooks. Rippon added the 4th verse of this hymn in 1787.

Oliver Holden was born near Boston, became a carpenter and real estate dealer by trade, and then became a Puritan clergyman. He also served as a Massachusetts state representative from 1818 to 1833. His love for music led to the publication of multiple hymn books. In 1792, he wrote the tune "Coronation" for this hymn. It was first published in Holden's 1793 publication "Union Harmony".

A later tune called "Diadem" was composed by James Ellor (1819-1899) in 1838. He was born in England and came to America at the age of 24. He was a hatmaker by trade with a natural musical talent.

Historical Setting For "ALL HAIL THE POWER OF JESUS' NAME"

The U.S. Mint was created in 1792, establishing the U.S. national coinage system.
Kentucky became a State in 1792.
France was the first country to adopt the Metric System in 1793.

All Hail the Power of Jesus' Name

Words by EDWARD PERRONET
Music by OLIVER HOLDEN

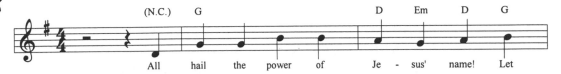

All hail the power of Je-sus' name! Let

an-gels pros-trate fall; Bring forth the roy-al

di - a - dem, And crown Him Lord of_____

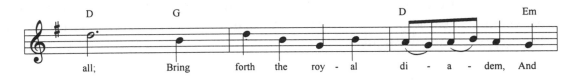

all; Bring forth the roy - al di - a - dem, And

crown Him Lord_____ of all!

When I Survey The Wondrous Cross

Words by: Isaac Watts (1674-1748) in 1707
Music from a Gregorian Chant
Arranged by: Lowell Mason (1792-1872) in 1824
Original Title: "Crucifixion To The World By The Cross Of Christ"
Scripture Reference: Galatians 6:14

Isaac Watts was born in Southampton, England, in 1674.   Watts displayed extraordinary talent in writing poetic verse at a young age. He was challenged by his father to "write something better for us to sing" than the usual metrical psalms, which were in use at the time in church services. Watts became the first Englishman to succeed in overcoming the prejudices that opposed the introduction of hymns into English public worship.   His hymns were strong and triumphant statements of Christian faith, and were about the only songs sang in churches through the 1700's.

Isaac Watts wrote this song in 1707 while preparing for a communion service. It appeared in print the same year, in Watts' first hymn collection "Hymns and Spiritual Songs". The hymn was originally titled " Crucifixion to the World by the Cross of Christ".

Lowell Mason arranged the hymn's tune, and gave it the name "Hamburg". Mason arranged the tune in 1824, from an old Gregorian Chant, the earliest church music known. After 1827 Mason devoted himself entirely to teaching and lecturing about music and was an enormous influence on church music in nineteenth-century America.

Historical Setting For "WHEN I SURVEY THE WONDROUS CROSS"

Charles Wesley was born the same year that Watts wrote this hymn, in 1707.
The United Kingdom of Great Britain was created in 1707 with the uniting of England and Scotland.
The Royal Society for the Prevention of Cruelty to Animals was founded in London in 1824.
A Supreme Court decision in 1824 freed U.S. rivers from monopoly control.

When I Survey the Wondrous Cross

Words by ISAAC WATTS
Music from a Gregorian chant

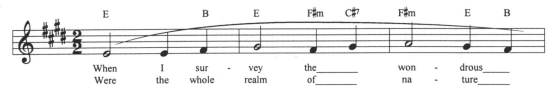

When I sur - vey the_____ won - drous_____
Were the whole realm of_____ na - ture_____

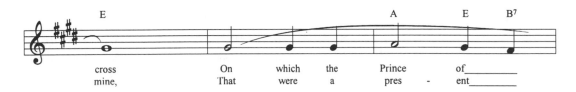

cross On which the Prince of_____
mine, That which were a pres - ent_____

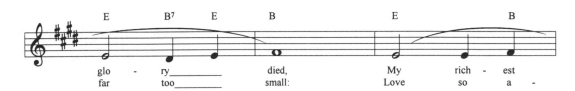

glo - ry_____ died, My rich - est
far too_____ small: Love so a -

gain I_____ count but_____ loss
maz - ing,_____ so de - vine,

And pour con - tempt on all my_____ pride.
De - mands my soul, my life my_____ all.

From Greenland's Icy Mountains

Words by: Reginald Heber (1783-1826) in 1819
Composed by: Lowell Mason (1792-1872) in 1824
Original Title: "Missionary Hymn"
Scripture Reference: Acts 16:9 Matthew 28:19-2O

Reginald Heber was born in Malpas, England. He became an Anglican missionary bishop in 1823, and a renowned writer of 57 hymns. This hymn, written in 1819, is considered to be the "theme song" for Protestant missionaries the world over since the 182O's. Heber composed the first three verses within fifteen minutes time, and the fourth verse probably within an hour, to be used as a hymn on Whitsunday. The song was written while Heber was a minister at Hodnet.

The words were first published in the "Evangelical Magazine" in July, 1821. Mary Howard of Savannah, Georgia came across the words and sent them to Lowell Mason to compose a tune.

Lowell Mason originally titled his tune name "Heber" in honor of the author, whom he never met. The tune name was revised and is now the "Missionary Hymn". Like the text, Mason was inspired to compose the music within a brief period of time in 1824.

It first appeared under the name "Missionary Hymn" in "The Boston Handel and Haydn Society Collection" of 1829.

Historical Setting For **"FROM GREENLAND'S ICY MOUNTAINS"**

Queen Victoria was born in 1819.

Washington Irving's classic stories "Rip Van Winkle" and "The Legend of Sleepy Hollow" were published in 1819.

Jedediah Strong Smith discovered the South Pass through the Rocky Mountains in 1824.

From Greenland's Icy Mountains

Words by REGINALD HEBER
Music by LOWELL MASON

1. From Greenland's icy mountains, From India's coral strand, Where Afric's sunny fountains Roll down their golden sand; From many an ancient river, From many a palmy plain, They call us to deliver Their land from error's chain.

2. What tho the spicy breezes
   Blow soft o'er Ceylon's isle;
   Tho ev'ry prospect pleases,
   And only man is vile;
   In vain with lavish kindness
   The gifts of God are strown;
   The heathen in his blindness
   Bows down to wood and stone.

We Are Climbing Jacob's Ladder

Author Unknown
Negro spiritual
Scripture Reference: Genesis 28:11-12

As with most spirituals and folk songs, there is no known author or composer of "Jacob's Ladder". Spirituals, like many folk songs, were spontaneously composed and spread by word of mouth, which allowed for changes in both words and melodies to occur.

This spiritual was first heard around 1825. The scriptural text is from Genesis 28:10-22.

Historical Setting For **"WE ARE CLIMBING JACOB'S LADDER"**

American Revolutionary hero, Lafayette, laid the cornerstone of the Bunker Hill Monument on the 50th anniversary of the battle in 1825.
The Erie Canal in New York State was completed in 1825.

Jacob's Ladder

Author unknown
Traditional Spiritual

1. We are climb - ing Ja - cob's

lad - der, We are climb - ing

Ja - cob's lad - er, We are

climb - ing Ja - cob's lad - er,

Child - ren of the Lord._____

2. Every round goes higher, higher...

3. Brother, do you love my Jesus?...

4. If you love Him, why not serve Him?...

5. We are climbing higher, higher...

Amazing Grace

Words by: John Newton (1725-1807) in 1779
Early American Melody from 1831
Original Title: "Faith's Review & Expectation"
Scripture Reference: Ephesians 2:8,9 John 9:25

John Newton was captain of a slave ship in 1748 before his conversion to Christianity, which came after a storm almost destroyed him and his human cargo. At age 39 he became an ordained minister, and a friend of William Cowper. The two men published the "Olney Hymns" collection in 1779 "for the use of plain people". The collection contained 349 hymns, of which 67 were written by Cowper.

Newton wrote nearly 300 poems during his life, with "Amazing Grace" being the best known. It first appeared in the "Olney Hymns" of 1779. John Newton wrote the first four stanzas of this hymn, and the 5th verse, beginning "When we've been there ten thousand years...", was added later by John P. Rees (1828-1900). The origin of the hymn's music, first published in Carrell and Clayton's "Virginia Harmony" of 1831, is not certain, but most authorities believe it to have originated in the rural southern United States. The tune name is "Amazing Grace".

Historical Setting For **"AMAZING GRACE"**

The capital of Virginia moved from Williamsburg to Richmond in 1779.
Sweet corn (grown by the Iroquois) is discovered in America in 1779.
The term "Old Glory" was first used to denote the U.S. flag in 1831.
The first known transportation of mail by railroad occurred in South Carolina in 1831.
The McCormick reaper was demonstrated by Cyrus Hall McCormick in 1831.

Amazing Grace

Words by JOHN NEWTON
Traditional American Melody

A Charge To Keep I Have

Words by: Charles Wesley (1707-1788) in 1762
Composed by: Lowell Mason (1792-1872) in 1832
Original Title: "Keep The Charge Of The Lord, That Ye Die Not"
Scripture Reference: Ephesians 4:1 Leviticus 8:35

Charles Wesley based this text on Leviticus 8:35. It first appeared in Wesley's "Short Hymns of Select Passages of Holy Scriptures", published in 1762. The original title was "Keep the Charge of the Lord, That Ye Die Not".

Lowell Mason is called the "Father of American Church and Public School Music". He was born in Medfield, Massachusetts. Mason composed this tune by the name "Boylston". The tune was first used with the text in the "Unison Collection of Church Music", published in 1832. In all, Mason is credited with composing and arranging approximately 700 hymn tunes.

Historical Setting For "A CHARGE TO KEEP I HAVE"

Benjamin Franklin made improvements to the harmonica and turned it into a practical musical instrument in 1762.

Mozart toured Europe as a musical prodigy at the age of six in 1762.

Charles Carroll, the last surviving signer of the Declaration of Independence, died in 1832.

Samuel Francis Smith wrote the patriotic song "America" in 1832.

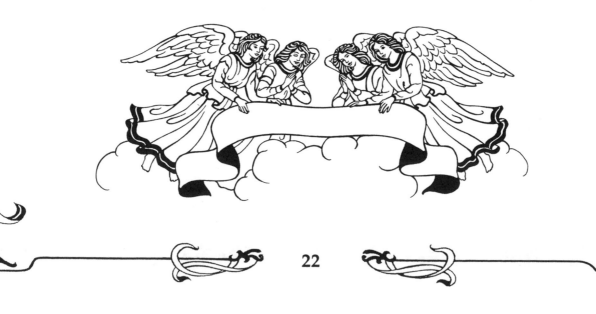

A Charge to Keep

Words by CHARLES WESLEY
Music by LOWELL MASON

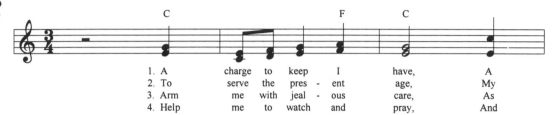

1. A charge to keep I have, A
2. To serve the pres - ent age, My
3. Arm me with jeal - ous care, As
4. Help me to watch and pray, And

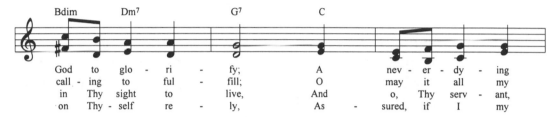

God to glo - ri - fy; A nev - er - dy - ing
call - ing to ful - fill; O may it all my
in Thy sight to live, And o, Thy serv - ant,
on Thy - self re - ly, As - sured, if I my

soul to save, And fit it for the sky.
pow'rs en - gage, To do my Mas - ter's will!
Lord, pre - pare, A strict ac - count to give!
trust be - tray, I shall for - ev - er die.

My Faith Looks Up To Thee

Words by: Ray Palmer (1808-1887) in 1830
Composed by: Lowell Mason (1792-1872) in 1832
Scripture Reference: Ephesians 3:12

Ray Palmer was born in Little Compton, Rhode Island. He was a descendant of John and Priscilla Alden, two of the Mayflower Pilgrims. Palmer was ordained a Congregational minister in 1835. He served as pastor of churches in Maine and New York.

Palmer wrote this hymn in New York in 1830, while serving as a school teacher, after a discouraging year in which he battled illness, loneliness and poverty. He said he had no thought of writing a hymn for Christian worship, but that "I composed them with a deep consciousness of my own need".

Palmer presented his text to his friend, Lowell Mason, in 1832. Mason told Palmer that he predicted Palmer would best be remembered for the writing of this hymn despite anything else he achieved in life.

Lowell Mason wrote the tune "Olivet" for this hymn, and it was printed in a hymnal called "Spiritual Songs For Social Worship" in 1832, edited by Mason and Tom Hastings.

Historical Setting For "MY FAITH LOOKS UP TO THEE"

Oliver Wendell Holmes published his poem "Old Ironsides" in 1830.

Cincinnati, Ohio was known as "Porkopolis" in 1830 because it was the leading meat-packing city in the U.S.

The first national convention for the nomination of a presidential candidate was held in 1832.

Abraham Lincoln was defeated in his first run for a public office in 1832.

My Faith Looks Up To Thee

Words by RAY PALMER
Music by LOWELL MASON

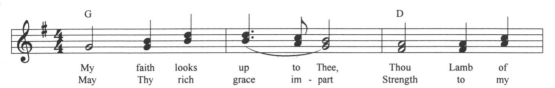

My faith looks up to Thee, Thou Lamb of
May Thy rich grace im - part Strength to my

Cal - va - ry, Sav - iour di - vine; Now hear me
faint - ing heart, My zeal in - spire; As Thou hast

when I pray, Take all my sin a - way,
died for me, O may my love to Thee,

O let me from this day Be whol - ly Thine!
Pure, warm, and change - less be, A liv - ing fire!

Rock Of Ages

Words by: Augustus Montague Toplady (1740-1778) in 1776
Composed by: Thomas Hastings (1784-1872) in 1832
Scripture Reference: I Corinthians 10:4 Psalms 94:22   Isaiah 26:4

Toplady was born in Surrey, England, and was converted to Christianity at age 16 under the Methodists. In 1762 he became a powerful and respected priest of the Anglican church. The strong and passionate lines in this hymn were written to refute some teachings by the Wesleys' with which Toplady did not agree.

"Rock of Ages" was published in "The Gospel Magazine" in 1776. Of the many hymns written by Toplady, this is the one for which he is known today. Due to frail health, Toplady died of overwork and tuberculosis at the age of 38.

Thomas Hastings was born in Washington, Connecticut. He was a self-taught church musician, who overcame the handicaps of being an albino. He is credited with composing over 1,000 hymn tunes, 600 complete hymns, and fifty collections of religious music. Hastings composed this tune in 1832 and published it in a songbook called "Spiritual Songs for Social Worship", in 1833. His tune name for this hymn is "Toplady".

Historical Setting For **"ROCK OF AGES"**

The Declaration of Independence was signed July 4 in Philadelphia in 1776. Philadelphia was the largest city in America at the time with 40,000 people.
Boston Baptist minister Samuel Francis Smith wrote the patriotic song "America" in 1832.
Atlanta, Georgia was founded by Hardy Ivy in 1833.

Rock of Ages

Words by AUGUSTUS M. TOPLADY
Music by THOMAS HASTINGS

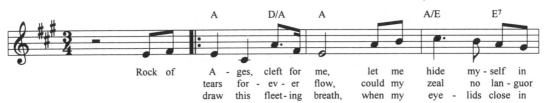

Rock of A - ges, cleft for me, let me hide my - self in
tears for - ev - er flow, could my zeal no lan - guor
draw this fleet - ing breath, when my eye - lids close in

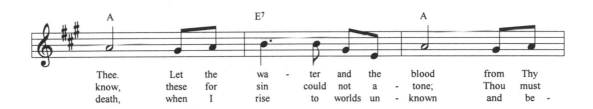

Thee. Let the wa - ter and the blood from Thy
know, these for sin could not a - tone; Thou must
death, when I rise to worlds un - known and be -

wound - ed side which flowed be of sin the dou - ble
save, and Thou a - lone. In my hand no price I
hold Thee on Thy throne, Rock of A - ges, cleft for

cure, save from wrath and make me pure. Could my
bring; sim - ply to Thy cross I cling. While I
me, let me to hide my - self in Thee.

Jesus, Lover Of My Soul

Words by: Charles Wesley (1707-1788) in 1738
Composed by: Simeon Buckley Marsh (1798-1875) in 1834
Original Title: "In Temptation"
Scripture Reference: Isaiah 32:22 Corinthians 1:3,5

This hymn is considered possibly the most famous of all 6,500 hymns that Wesley wrote. The words were penned in 1738 and first published in 1740, in the Wesley's hymnbook "Hymns and Sacred Poems", but it did not become a popular congregational hymn until after 1834, when Marsh composed his tune. John Wesley disliked the hymn for being "too sentimental", but it has now been translated into all the languages of the missionary world. If a person averaged out Charles Wesley's hymn production, it would equal three hymns a week over 57 years.

Simeon Marsh was born in Sherburne, New York. He was a devoted layman, and a devout teacher of singing. He organized several singing schools near Albany, New York. It was while on horseback, riding between two of these schools, that this melody came to him in 1834. His hymn tune name is "Martyn".

A later tune was composed by Joseph Parry (1841-1903). He was a Welsh-born music scholar and composer. His tune for this hymn is "Aberystwyth", composed in 1879.

Historical Setting For "JESUS, LOVER OF MY SOUL"

Cuckoo clocks originated in 1738. Umbrellas were first used in America in 1738.
The first American tinware peddlers (tinkers) began selling tin items door to door in Connecticut in 1740.
Brooklyn, New York, was chartered as a city in 1834.
28 million acres of U.S. public lands were offered for sale in 1834 and 1835.

Jesus, Lover of My Soul

Words by CHARLES WESLEY
Music by SIMEON B. MARSH

How Firm A Foundation

Words attributed to: "K"
Published by: John Rippon (1751-1836) in 1787
Early American Folk Music from 1837
Scripture Reference: Isaiah 43:1-7 Hebrews 13:5

The authorship of this hymn has remained a mystery. It first appeared in John Rippon's 1787 collection "A Selection of Hymns From The Best Authors". The music director in Rippon's church was named John Keene, so it has generally been thought that he was the author of the text, but it has never been confirmed.

Rippon served as the pastor of the Carter Lane Baptist Church in London for 63 years, beginning in 1775. He published many of his sermons and edited several hymnbooks.

The composer of this music is also unknown. It first appeared in William Caldwell's 1837 publication "Union Harmony". The song had been sung for many years to the tune of "Adeste Fideles" by John Francis Wade.

Historical Setting For **"HOW FIRM A FOUNDATION"**

The U.S. Constitution was created at Philadelphia's Independence Hall over a 16 week period in 1787.

Delaware, Pennsylvania and New Jersey became the first States in the U.S. in 1787.

The first canned foods were produced in 1787.

Michigan became a State in 1837.

The Texas Rangers, Procter & Gamble, and Tiffany & Co. all had their beginnings in 1837.

How Firm A Foundation

Author unknown

How firm a foun - da - tion, ye
"Fear not, I am with thee. O

saints_____ of the Lord, Is laid for your
be_____ not des - mayed, For I am thy

faith_____ in His ex - cel - lent Word! What
God;_____ I will still give thee aid. I'll

more can He say than to you,_____ He hath
strength - en thee, say help thee, and cause_____ thee to

TACET

said_____ To you,_____ who for re - fuge, to
stand,_____ Up - held_____ by My gra - cious, om -

Je - sus have fled?_____ To you,_____ who for
nip - o - tent hand_____ Up - held_____ by My

re - fuge, to Je - sus have fled?
gra - cious, om - nip - o - tent hand."

Oh, For A Thousand Tongues To Sing

Words by Charles Wesley (1707-1788) in 1739
Composed by: Carl Gotthilf Glaser (1784-1829) in 1828
Arranged by Lowell Mason (1792-1872) in 1839
Original Title: "For The Anniversary Day of One's Conversion"
Scripture Reference: Acts 4:12 Revelation 5:11

1t is generally agreed that Charles Wesley and Isaac Watts have been the two most influential writers of English hymnody to date. Wesley wrote nearly 6,500 hymn texts. This hymn was inspired by a chance remark made by a Moravian leader, Peter Bohler, to Charles Wesley. Bohler exclaimed, "Had I a thousand tongues, I would praise Christ Jesus with all of them." Wesley wrote this hymn on the anniversary of his Aldersgate Christian conversion experience and was published in his "Hymns and Sacred Poems" in 1739.

Carl Glaser was a German choral master and author of the tune "Azmon", in 1828, to which we sing this hymn. He was born in Weissenfels, Germany. He moved to Barmen and became a teacher of piano, violin and voice.

Lowell Mason arranged the tune as we know it today in 1839. Mason gave up a banking career at the age of 37 to become one of America's most influential music educators.

Historical Setting For **"OH, FOR A THOUSAND TONGUES TO SING"**

Noah Webster published his "American Dictionary of the English Language" in 1828. Telegraph pioneer Samuel F.B. Morse made the first Daguerreotype portraits to be produced in America in 1839.
English preacher, George Whitefield, arrived in America in 1739 to begin an evangelistic tour that was to help promote Methodism.

O, For a Thousand Tongues

Words and Music by,
CHARLES WESLEY
and CARL GLASER

Oh for a thou - sand tongues to sing my great Re - deem - er's praise, the glo - ries of my God and King, the_____ tri - umphs of His grace.

2. My gracious Master and my God,
   Assist me to proclaim,
   To spread through all the earth abroad
   The honors of Thy name.

3. Jesus! the name that charms our fears,
   That bids out sorrows cease;
   'Tis music in the sinner's ears,
   'Tis life, and health and peace.

4. He breaks the pow'r of canceled sin,
   He sets the prison'r free;
   His blood can make the foulest clean;
   His blood abailed for me.

5. Hear Him, ye deaf; His praise, ye dumb.
   Your loss'ned tongues employ;
   Ye blind, behold your Saviour come;
   And leap, ye lame, for joy.

Blest Be The Tie That Binds

Words by: John Fawcett (1740-1817) in 1772
Composed by: Hans Georg Naegeli (1773-1836)
Arranged by: Lowell Mason (1792-1872) in 1845
Original Title: "Brotherly Love"
Scripture Reference: Ephesians 4:3 Hosea 11:4

John Fawcett was born in Yorkshire, England. He became a Baptist clergyman and educator, ordained in 1763. Reverend Fawcett served the poor parish of Wainsgate, England for several years. In 1772, he almost left to serve a larger, wealthier church in London, but he elected to stay at Wainsgate because of the "tie that binds" friends together.

Fawcett's wife, Mary, told the Wainsgate congregation "we just cannot break the ties of affection that bind us to you dear friends". Rev. Fawcett went on to serve the little parish for a total of 54 years. He penned many sermons, essays, and over 150 hymns. This poem by Fawcett was written in 1772, and first published in 1782 under the title "Brotherly Love" in a collection of hymns, "Hymns Adapted to the Circumstance of Public Worship", to which he contributed 166 original hymns.

Hans Naegeli was born in Wetzikon, Switzerland. He established a music publishing firm at age 19, and founded the Swiss Association for the Cultivation of Music. His innovative methods of teaching music influenced Lowell Mason and others. Lowell Mason's 1845 arrangement of Naegeli's tune, "Dennis", provides the music familiar to us today. The tune first appeared in Mason's "The Psaltry; a New Collection of Church Music".

Historical Setting For **"BLEST BE THE TIE THAT BINDS"**

Joseph Priestley, an English clergyman-chemist, gave "rubber" its name in 1772.
The Great Seal of the United States was adopted in 1782.
James Watt invented a double-acting rotary steam engine in 1782 capable of driving machinery of all kinds.
Florida became the 27th State and Texas became the 28th State in 1845.
The United States Naval Academy was founded at Annapolis, Maryland in 1845.

Blest Be the Tie That Binds

Words by JOHN FAWCETT
Music by HANS G. NAEGELI

1. Blest be___ the tie___ that binds Our hearts___ in

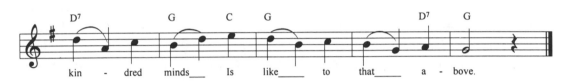

Chris - tian love; The fel - low - ship___ of

kin - dred minds___ Is like___ to that___ a - bove.

2. Before out Father's throne
   We pour our ardent prayers;
   Our fears, our hopes, our aims, are one,
   Our comforts and our cares.

3. We share our mutual woes,
   Our mutual burdens bear,
   And often for each other flows
   The sympathizing tear.

4. When we asunder part,
   It gives us inward pain;
   But we shall still be joined in heart,
   And hope to meet again.

Just As I Am

Words by: Charlotte Elliott (1789-1871) in 1834
Composed by: William B. Bradbury (1816-1868) in 1849
Original Title: "Him That Cometh To Me I Will In No Wide Cast Out"
Scripture Reference: John 6:37

Miss Elliott was born in Clapham, England. An illness at age 33 left her an invalid the rest of her 50 years. She wrote 150 hymns, including this one which she wrote while living in Brighton, England, in 1834. Elliott's hymn was published in 1841 in her "Invalid Hymn Book". She was inspired to write this hymn, dedicated to the handicapped and unwanted, by the biblical scripture of John 6:37.

This song has been sung repeatedly at Billy Graham crusades, when people are asked to come forward and give their lives to Jesus Christ. It quite possibly has influenced more people for Christ than any other song.

William Bradbury was born in York, Maine. He was a Baptist sacred music composer, and published 59 collections of sacred and secular music during his lifetime. Bradbury wrote the tune "Woodworth" in 1849, and it was joined with Elliott's text by Thomas Hastings, and published in "The Mendelssohn Collection" by Hastings and Bradbury. The song came into common use in the late 1860's.

Historical Setting For "JUST AS I AM"

The legend of Davy Crockett grew from the publication of his autobiography, The Life of David Crockett, in 1834.

U.S. President, William Henry Harrison, died from pneumonia in 1841, after only one month in office.

Composer, Robert Schumann, completed his Opus 38 in 1841.

The nation had gold fever, as the California Gold Rush sent people streaming west in 1849.

Just As I Am

Words by CHARLOTTE ELLIOTT
Music by WILLIAM B. BRADBURY

Just___ as I am___ with -
Just___ as I am___ Thou

out___ one plea, But that___ Thy blood was
wilt___ re - ceive, Wilt that wel - come, par - don,

shed for me; And___ that Thou bidd'st___ me come to Thee,___ O
cleanse re - lieve; Be - cause Thy prom - ise I be - lieve,___ O

Lamb of God,___ I come, I come!
Lamb of God,___ I come, I come!

Fairest Lord Jesus

Unknown Author
Arranged by: Richard Storrs Willis (1819-1900) in 1850
Scripture Reference: Colossians 1:16 Song of Solomon 6:10

This song dates from 1662. The text, titled "Schonster Herr Jesu", first appeared in the Roman Catholic "Munster Gesangbuch" of 1677. Later, a man named, Hoffman Fallersleben, heard a group of Silesians (Silesia is now part of Poland) singing the hymn and he published the words and music in his "Schlesische Volkslieder" in 1842. This is the form in which we now know the hymn.

No one is sure who first translated the text from German into English. The 4th verse was translated by Joseph A. Seiss (1823-1904) and his version titled "Beautiful Savior" was first published in "The Sunday School Book" of the American Lutheran General Council in Philadelphia in 1873.

Richard Willis was born in Boston. He was a Catholic music critic, and published several collections of hymns. Willis arranged this hymn in 1850, and he titled the tune "Crusader's Hymn", from the "Schlesische Volkslieder" in 1842. The hymn first appeared in Willis' "Church Chorals and Choir Studies". Willis is also known for the hymn tune "Carol" used with "It Came Upon A Midnight Clear."

Historical Setting For **"FAIREST LORD JESUS"**

Puritans became known as "Nonconformists" in England in 1662.
The first dinosaur bones were discovered in 1677.
Elijah White led the first large wagon train of 120 people down the newly mapped Oregon Trail in 1842.
Up till 1850 only half the children born in the U.S. would reach the age of five.

Fairest Lord Jesus

Author unknown

1. Fair - est Lord Je - sus! Rul - er of all

na - ture! O Thou of God and____

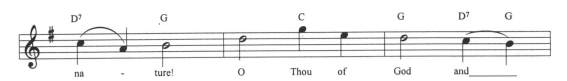

man the Son! Thee will I

cher - ish, Thee will I hon - or, Thou

my soul's glo - ry, joy, and crown.

2. Fair are the meadows,
   Fairer still the woodlands,
   Robed in the blooming garb of spring;
   Jesus is fairer, Jesus is purer,
   Who makes the woeful heart to sing.

3. Fair is the sunshine,
   Fairer still the moonlight,
   And all the twinkling starry host;
   Jesus shines brighter,
   Jesus shines purer,
   Than all the angels heav'n can boast!

Gloria Patri

English Translation by: John Mason Neale (1818-1866) in 1851
Composed by: Charles Meineke (1782-1850) in 1844
Scripture Reference: Ephesians 5:20 Matthew 28:19

Charles Meineke was born in Germany, and emigrated to America in 1810. He became the organist for St. Paul's Episcopal Church in Baltimore in 1836 and published several volumes of hymn tunes during his life.

This doxology hymn, composed in 1844, begins "Glory Be to the Father...". It is known as the "Lesser Doxology", in order to distinguish it from "Gloria in Excelsis", the "Greater Doxology". The completed text, as we know it, dates back to the time of St. Thomas Aquinas in the early 16th century, with the English translation rendered by John Mason Neale in 1851.

Neale was deeply interested in the hymns of the Latin and Greek churches. He served as the warden at Sackville College in East Grinstead, England from 1846 until his death.

Another popular tune composition for "Gloria Patri" was by Henry Wellington Greatorex (1813-1858), from his "Collection of Church Music" in 1851. Greatorex was born in Burton-on-Trent, England and came to America in 1839. He came from a family noted through several generations for their musical ability. He served as an organist in various churches from 1839 till his death from yellow fever in 1858.

Historical Setting For "GLORIA PATRI"

Polka dancing was introduced to America in New York in 1844.
The YMCA was founded in London by George Williams in 1844.
The railroad caboose car originated about 1851 with the New York & Erie Railroad.

Gloria Patri

English translation by JOHN M, NEALE
Music by CHARLES MEINEKE

Glo - ry be to the Fa - ther, and to the

Son, and to the Ho - y Ghost; As it

was in the be - gin - ning, is

now, and ev - er shall be, world with - out

end. A - men, A - men.

A Mighty Fortress Is Our God

Written & Composed by: Martin Luther (1483-1546) in 1529
English translation by: Frederick Henry Hedge (1805-1890) in 1853
Original German Title: "Ein'Feste Burg ist Unser Gott"
Scripture Reference: Psalm 46, 2 Samuel 22:2

Martin Luther is known as the "Father of the German Reformation". He was also a skilled hymn writer, and is credited with writing 37 hymns. He wrote "A Mighty Fortress", his best known hymn, 12 years after he began the Protestant Reformation with the posting of the 95 theses (complaints) on the doors of the Cathedral of Wittenberg, Germany in 1517. Luther turned his interest to music in 1524 with the publication of a hymn book. His musical abilities, which included the playing of the flute and the lute, led to the introduction of hymns for congregational use. Luther wrote that "music is a gift and grace of God, not an invention of men...it makes people cheerful...then one forgets all wrath, impurity and other devices."

"A Mighty Fortress" is the oldest of our favorite Protestant hymns, written in 1529, for the Diet of Spires. (The term "Protestant" was first used that same year.) The hymn became the great rallying cry of the Reformation, and is known as the "Battle Hymn of the Reformation". Luther titled the tune for this hymn "Ein' Feste Burg", first published in Klug's "Gesangbuch" of 1529.

Rev. Frederick Hedge was a New England clergyman, born in Cambridge, Massachusetts, and was ordained a Unitarian minister in 1829. He served several New England churches while teaching ecclesiastical history and German at Harvard. In 1853, he published "Hymns for the Church of Christ", which included his translation of this centuries old, but ever popular hymn.

Historical Setting For **"A MIGHTY FORTRESS"**

Lutherans were first called "Protestants" in 1529. This resulted from their protests against Catholic decisions.

Cocoa had just been introduced to Europe in 1529. Spanish explorer, Hernando Cortez, learned of the drink from the Aztecs.

The potato chip was invented in 1853 by George Crum.

The Territory of Washington was formed in 1853 after separation from the Oregon Territory.

A Mighty Fortress is Our God

by MARTIN LUTHER
English translation by FREDERICK H. HEDGE

A might-y fort-ress is our God, A
And tho' this world, with dev-ils filled, Should

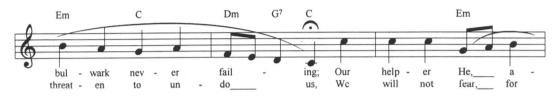

bul-wark nev-er fail-ing; Our help-er He,____ a-
threat-en to un-do____ us, We will not fear,____ for

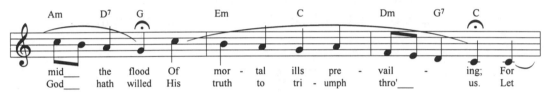

mid____ the flood Of mor-tal ills pre-vail-ing; For
God____ hath willed His truth to tri-umph thro'____ us. Let

still our an-cient foe Doth seek to work his
goods and kin-dred go, This mor-tal life al-

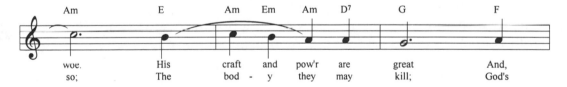

woe. His craft and pow'r are great And,
so; The bod-y they may kill; God's

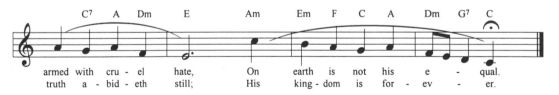

armed with cru-el hate, On earth is not his e-qual.
truth a-bid-eth still; His king-dom is for-ev-er.

'Tis Midnight and On Olive's Brow

Words by: William Bingham Tappan (1794-1849) in 1822
Composed by: William B. Bradbury (1816-1868) in 1853
Scripture Reference: Mark 14:12,35-36 John 19:30

William Tappan was orphaned at the age of twelve. He practiced the trade of clockmaking until 1822, when a growing interest in the Sunday school movement led to his employment as the Superintendent of the American Sunday School Union. In 1849 Tappan was ordained as a Congregational minister.

Tappan was also a prolific poet, publishing ten volumes of verse, of which only this one, written and published in "Poems" in 1822, became a hymn. Prolific composer, William Bradbury, composed the tune "Olive's Brow" for this hymn in 1853.

Historical Setting For **"TIS MIDNIGHT AND ON OLIVE'S BROW"**

The Royal Academy of Music, London, was founded in 1822.
Franz Liszt made his debut as a pianist in Vienna at the age of 11 in 1822.
The first false teeth patent was granted in 1822.
Henry Steinway and sons began manufacturing pianos in New York in 1853.
Stephen Collins Foster published "My Old Kentucky Home, Good Night" in 1853.

'Tis Midnight; and On Olive's Brow

Words by WILLIAM B. TAPPAN
Music by WILLIAM B. BRADBURY

1. 'Tis mid - night; and on Ol - ive's brow The
2. 'Tis mid - night; and from all re - moved The
3. 'Tis mid - night; and for oth - er's guilt The
4. 'Tis mid - night; and from e - ther - plains Is

star is dimmed that late - ly shone; 'Tis
Sav - ior wrest - les 'lone with fears; E'en
Man of Sor - rows weeps in blood; Yet
borne the song that an - gels know; Un -

mid - night; in the gar - den now The
that dis - ci - ple whom He loved Heeds
He, who hath in an - guish knelt, Is
heard by mor - tals are the strains That

suff - 'ring Sav - ior prays a - lone.
not his Mast - er's grief and tears.
not for - sak - en by His God.
sweet - ly soothe the Sav - ior's woe.

Oh Happy Day

Words by Philip Doddridge (1702-1751) in 1755
Composed by: Edward Francis Rimbault (1816-1876) in 1854
Original Title: "Rejoicing In Our Covenant Engagement To God"
Scripture Reference: Isaiah 61:10 Psalm 56 2 Chronicles 15:12-14

Philip Doddridge was the youngest of twenty children (eighteen of which died in infancy) and was orphaned at 13. He became an English Nonconformist clergyman at Northampton in 1739, where he served the rest of his life.

Doddridge was a prolific writer of hymns, and a friend of Isaac Watts and the Wesley brothers. He is considered one of England's finest 18th century hymn writers. All of his 400 hymn texts, including this one, were published posthumously in 1755. The text for this song was based on Psalm 56. It was originally titled "Rejoicing in Our Covenant Engagement to God".

Edward Rimbault was born in London, England. He served as an organist in a number of London churches and was a noted musicologist and scholar. He also published a variety of music, including madrigals, ballads, and sacred. Rimbault is credited with the refrain melody for this hymn, adapted from a popular song titled "Happy Land". The composer of the music for the verses is unknown.

The completed tune first appeared in "The Wesleyan Sacred Harp" by William McDonald, published in Boston in 1854. McDonald is credited with adding the words for the refrain "Happy day, happy day, when Jesus washed my sins away". Another century later, the Edwin Hawkins Singers popularized the song, in 1969.

Historical Setting For "OH HAPPY DAY"

The year 1755 marked the beginning of English and French hostilities in North America with the seizure of 300 French ships by the English. This conflict is known as the Seven Years War.

In 1755, 100,000 acres of land were purchased in southern Carolina to serve as the first Jewish settlement in America.

"Jeannie With The Light Brown Hair" was published by Stephen Foster in 1854.

The "hoopskirt" became the latest feminine wardrobe addition in 1854.

Oh Happy Day

Words by PHILIP DODDRIDGE
Music by EDWARD F. RIMBAULT

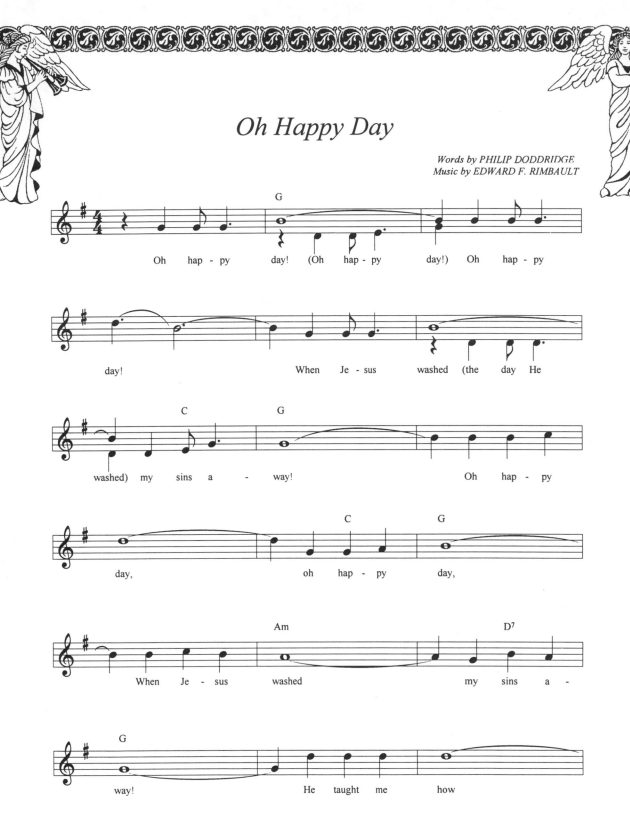

Oh Happy Day

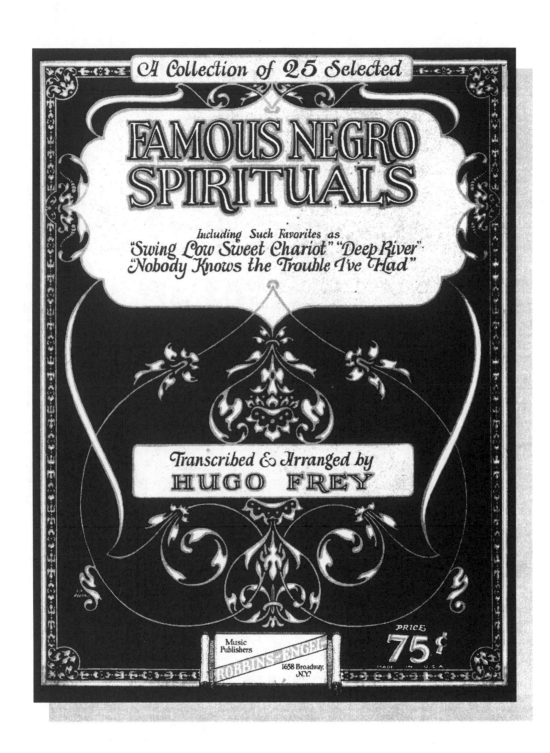

Copyright 1924
This is one of the first books to contain
the most popular Spirituals of the day
into piano and vocal arrangements.

The Church In The Wildwood

Written & Composed by William Savage Pitts (1830-1918) in 1857
Alternate Title: "The Little Brown Church In The Vale"
2 Chronicles 30:8

This hymn is also known as "The Little Brown Church In The Vale". The location of the church, and the setting for the song, is located near Nashua, Iowa. Dr. Pitts wrote the hymn in 1857 after visiting the area where the church was later to be built.

He returned in 1863 during its construction and then had the hymn published in 1865.   The construction of this famous church building began in 1860, but was suspended due to the Civil War, and not completed until 1864.
At this time Dr. Pitts was teaching music at nearby Bradford Academy. At the dedication of the new church building, his singing class from the academy sang this song for the first time. The church was originally painted brown, because that was the cheapest paint at the time. It has become a favorite site for weddings over the years. The Little Brown Church in the Vale has special meaning for this author, because my parents were married there in 1936.

In 1865, Pitts sold the song to a Chicago music publisher for twenty-five dollars. The money helped Pitts enroll in Rush Medical College. After graduation in 1868 Pitts practiced medicine in Fredricksburg, Iowa until his retirement in 1906.

Historical Setting For **"THE CHVRCH IN THE WILDWOOD"**

The first Currier & Ives prints were issued in 1857.
"We Three Kings" by John Henry Hopkins was written in 1857.
Abraham Lincoln was assassinated in 1865.
The Pullman railroad sleeping cars were introduced in 1865.

The Church in the Wildwood

Words and Music by
WILLIAM S. PITTS

There's a church in the val - ey by the wild - wood, no

love - li - er spot in the dale. No_____ place is so dear to my

child - hood as the lit - tle brown church in the vale. Oh_____

come, come, come, come, come to the church in the wild - wood. Oh

come to the church in the vale. No_____ spot is so dear to my

child - hood as the lit - tle brown church in the vale.

Saviour, Like A Shepherd Lead Us

Words ascribed to: Dorothy Ann Thrupp (1779-1847) in 1836
Composed by: William B. Bradbury (1816-1868) in 1859
Scripture Reference: Psalm 32:8 John 10:2-4

Dorothy Thrupp was born and lived in London, England. She was a prolific writer of children's hymns, although she seldom signed her name to her works. When she did, she used a pseudonym, Iota. Because of this, it has never been fully proven that she was the actual author of this hymn. (The lyrics have also been attributed to Henry F. Lyte.) The poem first appeared in her 1836 collection "From Hymns for the Young" which she began compiling in 1830.

William Bradbury wrote the tune "Bradbury" for his 1859 publication "Oriola", a Sunday-school songbook.

Historical Setting For **"SAVIOUR, LIKE A SHEPHERD LEAD US"**

The Alamo fell to Santa Anna in 1836.
Narcissa Whitman was the first white woman to cross the North American Continent in 1836.
The popular song "Dixie" was performed for the first time in 1859.
Mason jars began using paraffin wax as a seal to preserve food in 1859.

Saviour, Like a Shepherd Lead Us

Words by DOROTHY A. THRUPP
Music by WILLIAM B. BRADBURY

Sav - iour like___ a___ Shep - herd lead us, Much we need Thy ten - der
We are Thine___ do___ Thou be - friend us, Be the Guard - ian of our

care; In Thy pleas - ant pas - tures feed us,_____
way; Keep Thy flock, from sin de - fend us,_____

For our use Thy folds pre - pare. Bless - ed Je - sus, Bless - ed
Seek us when we go a - stray. Bless - ed Je - sus, Bless - ed

Je - sus, Thou hast bought us, Thine we are; Bless - ed
Je - sus, Hear Thy chil - dren when they pray; Bless - ed

Je - sus, Bless - ed Je - sus, Thou hast bought us, Thine we are.
Je - sus, Bless - ed Je - sus, Hear Thy chil - dren when they pray.

Nearer, My God, To Thee

Words by: Sarah Flower Adams (1805-1848) in 1840
Composed by: Lowell Mason (1792-1872) in 1859
Scripture Reference: Genesis 28:11-12

Sarah Adams was born in Harlow, Essex, and married William Adams in 1834. She was an English writer of verse, prose, and even a catechism. It is recorded that the band on the Titanic played her hymn as the ship sank in 1912.

Sarah wrote this hymn after studying Genesis 28:10-22, in 1840. The hymn was published in "Hymns and Anthems" by Reverend William Johnson Fox in 1841, and became known in America in 1844, but did not gain real popularity until it was matched with Mason's composition. Sarah's sister, Elizabeth, composed the original melody for this hymn and a number of melodies for her sister's song texts. Both Sarah and Eliza died from tuberculosis at young ages, within five years of this hymn's publication.

Lowell Mason wrote the melody "Bethany" the next morning after a sleepless night in 1859. It first appeared in Mason's "The Sabbath Hymn and Tune Book" in 1859.

Historical Setting For **"NEARER, MY GOD, TO THEE"**

The Rainer Family, a mixed quartet of Swiss singers, were entertaining American audiences throughout the United States in 1840 with the mountain songs of their native land. One song they helped introduce to America was "Silent Night".
The U.S. population was slightly over 17 million in 1840.
Hypnosis was discovered by Scottish surgeon James Baird in 1841.
Samuel Morse transmitted the first telegraph message in 1844.
Oregon was admitted as the 33rd State in 1859.
The first oil well in the U.S. was opened in Titusville, Pennsylvannia in 1859.

Nearer, My God, to Thee

Words by SARAH F. ADAMS
Music by LOWELL MASON

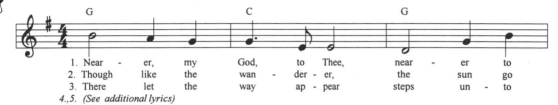

1. Near - er, my God, to Thee, near - er to
2. Though like the wan - der - er, the sun go
3. There let the way ap - pear steps un - to

4.,5. (See additional lyrics)

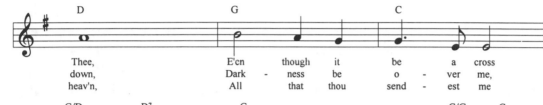

Thee, E'en though it be a cross
down, Dark - ness be o - ver me,
heav'n, All that thou send - est me

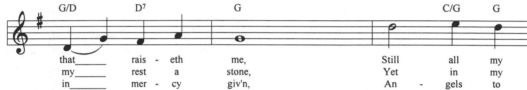

that_____ rais - eth me, Still all my
my_____ rest a stone, Yet in my
in_____ mer - cy giv'n, An - gels to

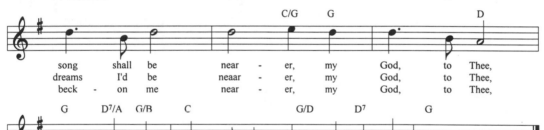

song shall be near - er, my God, to Thee,
dreams I'd be neaar - er, my God, to Thee,
beck - on me near - er, my God, to Thee,

Near - er, my God, to Thee, near - er to Thee.

4. Then with my waking thoughts bright with Thy praise,
Out of my stony griefs, Bethel I'll raise;
So by my woes to be nearer, my God, to Thee,
Nearer, my God, to Thee, nearer to Thee.

5. Or if on joyful wing, clearing the sky,
Sun, mood and stars forgot, upward I'll fly,
Still all my song shall be nearer, my God, to Thee,
Nearer, my God, to Thee, nearer to Thee.

Abide With Me

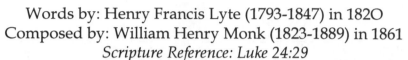

Words by: Henry Francis Lyte (1793-1847) in 1820
Composed by: William Henry Monk (1823-1889) in 1861
Scripture Reference: Luke 24:29

Henry Lyte was born in Scotland and was orphaned at an early age. He first became an Anglican pastor in 1815 and served parishes in Ireland and England. He battled tuberculosis all of his life, and for a long time, the words to this hymn were thought to have been written shortly before the death of Rev. Lyte. However, the stanzas are believed to have been written in 1820, after Lyte had visited a dying friend. The scriptural basis for the lyrics comes from Luke 24:29. The words were published in 1850, in a volume of Lyte's "Remains", published after his death. Lyte wrote a total of 80 hymn texts.

William Monk was an Anglican Church organist at the St. Matthias Church in Stoke Newington, England, from 1852 to 1889. He wrote the tune "Eventide" for this hymn in ten minutes. Monk composed many tunes for England's best known hymnal "Hymns Ancient and Modern" which sold 60 million copies. Monk's original tune for this hymn was called "Evening", composed in 1847 after he and his wife had watched a sunset, but he revised it in 1861.

Historical Setting For **"ABIDE WITH ME"**

Maine was admitted as the 23rd State in 1820.
Nathaniel Hawthorne published his novel "The Scarlet Letter" in 1850.
There were 31,799 miles of railroad in the U.S. in 1861.
Kansas became the 34th State in 1861.

Abide with Me

Words by HENRY F. LYTE
Music by WILLIAM H. MONK

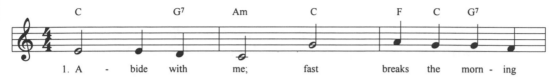

1. A - bide with me; fast breaks the morn - ing

light; Our day star ris - es,

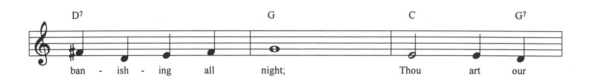

ban - ish - ing all night; Thou art our

strength, O Truth that mak - eth free,

We would un - fail - ing - ly a - bide in Thee.

2. I know no fear, with Thee at hand to bless,
   Sin hath no power and life no wretchedness;
   Health, hope, and love in all around I see,
   For those who trustingly abide in Thee.

3. I know Thy presence every passing hour,
   I know Thy peace, for Thou alone art power;
   O love divine, abiding constantly,
   I need not plead, Thou dost abide with me.

Holy, Holy, Holy

Words by: Reginald Heber (1783-1826)
Composed by: John Bacchus Dykes(1823-1876) in 1861
Scripture Reference: Revelation 4:8-11 Isaiah 6:3

Reginald Heber was born in Malpas, England. He became an Anglican missionary bishop and hymn writer. Some say he was "the greatest writer of English hymns since Charles Wesley".

He edited a publication called "Hymns Written and Adapted to the Weekly Church Services of the Year", which did much to popularize the singing of hymns. As a result, he has been described as "the Creator of the Modern Church Hymnbook".

This hymn came from his 1827 collection, published one year after his death by his widow and friends as a tribute to him. He actually wrote this text for Trinity Sunday (which occurs eight weeks after Easter) at the Hodnet parish in England, during the time he was vicar there from 1807 to 1823.

John Dykes became an Anglican clergyman in 1848 and is one of the best-remembered Victorian composers. This is one of nearly 300 hymn tunes credited to him. He named this hymn tune "Nicaea" after the church council of 325 A.D. It was published in 1861 in "Hymns Ancient and Modern...with Accompanying Tunes".

Historical Setting For "HOLY, HOLY, HOLY"

New Orleans held its first Mardi Gras celebration in 1827.
Audubon began his publication of drawings "The Birds of America" in 1827.
Abraham Lincoln became the 16th President of the United States in 1861.
Transcontinental telegraph service was established in the United States in 1861.

Holy, Holy, Holy

Words by REBINALD HEBER
Music by JOHN B. DYKES

1. Ho - ly, Ho - ly, Ho - ly, Lord, God Al -

might - y! Ear - ly in the morn - ing our

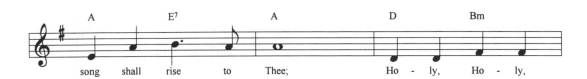

song shall rise to Thee; Ho - ly, Ho - ly,

Ho - ly! Mer - ci - ful and Might - y!

God in Three Per - sons, bless - ed Trin - i - ty!

2. Holy, Holy, Holy, All saints adore Thee,
   Casting down their golden crowns around the glassy sea;
   Cherubim and Seraphim,
   Falling down before Thee,
   Who wert and art and evermore shall be.

3. Holy, Holy, Holy, Lord God Almighty!
   All Thy work shall praise Thy name in earth and sky and sea;
   Holy, Holy, Holy, Merciful and Mighty!
   God in Three Persons, blessed Trinity!

Sweet Hour Of Prayer

Words by: William W. Walford (1772-1850) in 1842
Composed by: William Batchelder Bradbury (1816-1868) in 1861
Scripture Reference: Ephesians 6:18 I Thessalonians 5:17

Williiam Walford was a blind lay preacher and owner of a trinket shop in Coleshill, England. His lyrics, said to have been written in 1842, were transported to New York by the Rev. Thomas Salmon, of Coleshill. Salmon had the verses published in the "New York Observer", on September 13, 1845. (It should be noted, though, that it has never been absolutely confirmed that Walford was the actual writer of this hymn's text.)

The poem came to the attention of William Bradbury, and he composed the tune "Prayer" for the hymn. It was published in a book entitled "Church Melodies" in 1859. In 1861, Bradbury revised his tune for this hymn and titled it "Sweet Hour". The revised tune was published in his "Golden Chain" collection.

Bradbury had been a student in Lowell Mason's singing classes in Boston. He published more than 50 songbooks in his life.

Historical Setting For "SWEET HOUR OF PRAYER"

Ether began to be used as surgical anesthesia in 1842.
The polka came into fashion in the U.S. in 1842.
The U.S. Naval Academy opened at Annapolis in 1845.
Alexander Cartwright drew up a set of rules and organized the first baseball club, The Knickerbockers, in 1845.
The popular song "Dixie" was composed in 1859.
The U.S. population was at 32 million in 1861.

Sweet Hour of Prayer

Words by WILLIAM W. WALFORD
Music by WILLIAM B. BRADBURY

Sweet hour of prayer, sweet hour of prayer, That
hour of prayer, sweet hour of prayer, Thy

calls me from___ a world of care, And bids me at my
wings shall my___ pe - ti - tion bear To Him whose truth and

Fa - ther's throne Make all my wants___ and wish - es known. In
faith - ful - ness En - gage the wait - ing soul to bless. And

sea - sons of dis - tress and grief, My soul has of - ten
since He bids me seek His face, Be - lieve His Word and

found re - lief And oft es - caped the tempt - er's snare By
trust His grace, I'll cast on Him my ev - 'ry care And

thy re - turn,___ sweet hour of prayer. Sweet
wait for thee,___ sweet   hour of prayer.

Jesus Loves Me

Words by: Anna Bartlett Warner (1820-1915) in 1860
Composed by: William B. Bradbury (1816-1868) in 1861
Scripture Reference: Luke 18:17   Ephesians 3:17-18

Anna Warner was born on Long Island, New York. She was the daughter of a prominent New York lawyer, and never married. She lived with her sister and father near the U.S. West Point Military Academy.

"Jesus Loves Me" was a poem included in a novel "Say and Seal", written in 1860, and co-authored with her sister, Susan. Between them, the sisters wrote more than seventy books. They also taught a Sunday school class for West Point cadets in their home. This hymn has probably influenced more children for Christ than any other.

William Bradbury published 59 collections of sacred and secular music. Bradbury wrote the refrain to "Jesus Loves Me". He wrote the tune "China" for this hymn in 1861, and it appeared in his collection "The Golden Sower" in 1862.

Historical Setting For "JESUS LOVES ME"

The Pony Express flourished for only one year, in 1860.
The Winchester rifle was invented in 1860.
The estimated population of the U.S. at the beginning of the Civil War was 32.4 million.
The transcontinental telegraph put the Pony Express out of business in 1861.
The United States issued its first paper money in 1862.
The Homestead Act took effect in 1862.

Jesus Loves Me

Words by ANNA B. WARNER
Music by WILLIAM B. BRADBURY

1. Je - sus loves me! This I know, For the Bi - ble

tells me so; Lit - tle ones to Him be - long;

They are weak, but He is strong. Yes, Je - sus

loves me! Yes, Je - sus loves me!

Yes, Je - sus loves me! The Bi - ble tells me so.

2. Jesus from His throne on high,
   Came into this world to die;
   That I might from sin be free,
   Bled and died upon the tree.

3. Jesus loves me! He who died
   Heaven's gates to open wide,
   He will wash away my sin,
   Let His little child come in.

4. Jesus take this heart of mine;
   Make it pure and wholly Thine;
   Thou hast bled and died for me,
   I will henceforth live for Thee.

The Solid Rock

Words by: Edward Mote (1797-1874) in 1834
Composed by: William B. Bradbury (1816-1868) in 1863
Original Title: "The Immutable Basis of a Sinner's Hope"
Scripture Reference: I Corinthians 3:11 Matthew 7:25-26

Edward Mote was born in London, England, and converted to Christianity at the age of 16. He was a British cabinet maker, and writer of over 100 hymns. In 1836, Mote published a collection titled "Hymns of Praise, A New Selection of Gospel Hymns", in which he included "The Solid Rock", written in 1834.

Regarding the writing of this hymn Mote said "one morning it came into my mind as I went to labor to write a hymn on the experience of a Christian". The hymn was first sung at the bedside of a dying parishioner. It first appeared on a leaflet inserted in the "Spiritual Magazine". In 1852, Mote became a Baptist minister at the Strict Baptist Church and served the village of Horsham, Sussex in that capacity until 1873.

William Batchelder Bradbury composed the tune "Solid Rock" for this hymn in 1863. Bradbury was one of the foremost composers of early, American gospel music, and contributed to a large number of our favorite hymns. Bradbury's home was located in New York City, but he spent two years in Germany studying music under the finest teachers there.

Historical Setting For **"THE SOLID ROCK"**

Abraham Lincoln entered into politics at the age of 25 in 1834.
Abraham Lincoln gave his Gettysburg Address in 1863.
American automaker, Henry Ford, was born in 1863.
James Madison died at the age of 85 in 1836.

The Solid Rock

Words by EDWARD MOTE
Music by WILLIAM B. BRADBURY

1. My hope is built on noth - ing less, Than Je - sus' blood and right - eous - ness; I dare not trust the sweet - est frame, But whol - ly lean on Je - sus' name.
2. When dark - ness veils His love - ly face, I rest on His un - chang - ing grace; In ev - 'ry high and storm - y gale, My an - chor holds with - in the veil.
3. His oath, His cov - e - nant, His blood, Sup - port me in the whelm - ing flood; When all a - round my soul gives way, He then is all my hope and stay.
4. When He shall come with trum - pet sound, Oh, may I then in Him be found; Dressed in His right - eous - ness a - lone, Fault - less to stand be - fore the throne.

REFRAIN

On Christ, the sol - id Rock, I stand; All oth - er ground is sink - ing sand, All oth - er ground is sink - ing sand.

For The Beauty Of The Earth

Words by: Folliott Sandford Pierpoint (1835-1917) in 1864
Composed by: Conrad Kocher (1786-1872) in 1838
Original Title: "The Sacrifice of Praise"
Scripture Reference: Philippians 4:8 Isaiah 6:4

Folliott Pierpoint was born in Bath, England. He wrote this hymn in 1864, while enjoying the scenery around his native city. It's based on the text from the biblical book of James, "Every good gift is from above".

Pierpoint wrote the hymn specifically for a Church of England communion service.

Hymnal editors later altered some lines of the song to make it more usable in general praise. Pierpoint became an English classics instructor and hymnwriter. He wrote seven volumes of poems and hymn texts, but only this one remains in today's hymnals.

Conrad Kocher was born in Dietzingen, Germany. He made church choral music the major interest of his career, and studied music in Russia and Italy. In 1821 he founded the School of Sacred Song in Stuttgart, and held the position of organist at Stifts Church in Stuttgart from 1827 to 1865.

Kocher wrote the tune "Dix" in 1838 when it was published by him in a collection of chorals. His tune was joined with this hymn text in 1864 in "Lyra Eucharistica". Kocher did much to popularize four-part singing in churches.

Historical Setting For **"FOR THE BEAUTY OF THE EARTH"**

Music was introduced into public schools by Lowell Mason in 1838.
General Ulysses S. Grant became Commander-in-Chief of the Union armies in 1864.

For the Beauty of the Earth

Words by FOLLIOTT S. PIERPOINT
Music by CONRAD KOCHER

1. For the beau-ty of the earth, For the glo-ry of the skies, For the love which from our birth O-ver and a-round us lies; Lord of all, to Thee we raise This out hymn of grate-ful praise.

2. For the beauty of each hour,
Of the day and of the night,
Hill and vale, and tree and flow'r,
Sun and moon and stars of light:
Lord of all, to Thee we raise
This our hymn of grateful praise.

3. For the joy of ear and eye,
For the heart and mind's delight,
For the mystic harmony
Linking sense to sound and sight:

4. For the joy of human love,
Brother, sister, parent, child,
Friends on earth and friends above;
For all gentle tho'ts and mild:

He Leadeth Me

Words by: Joseph Henry Gilmore (1834-1918) in 1862
Composed by: William B. Bradbury (1816-1868) in 1864
Scripture Reference: Psalm 23:1-3

Joseph Gilmore was born in Boston, Massachusetts. He became a Baptist clergyman in 1862, and an English literature teacher at the University of Rochester from 1868 to 1911.

Gilmore hurriedly wrote the words for this hymn in 1862 while visiting with friends in the home of Deacon Wattson after preaching in the First Baptist Church of Philadelphia about the truths of Psalm 23. When Gilmore returned home he gave the hymn to his wife and forgot about it.

His wife sent it to "The Watchman and Reflector", a weekly paper, which published it in December of 1862. Three years later Dr. Gilmore was in Rochester, N.Y. to preach. When he opened a hymnal in the church, he found his hymn with a tune which had been composed by William Batchelder Bradbury.

William Bradbury was a leading contributor to the development of early gospel music in America. He was a pioneer in children's music for church and public schools. He published his composition for this hymn in 1864 in his collection "The Golden Censer". The tune name is "He Leadeth Me".

Historical Setting For **"HE LEADETH ME"**

The speed of light was successfully measured in 1862.
The Gatling gun was invented in 1862.
Stephen Foster, American songwriter, died in 1864.
Nevada became the 36th State in 1864.

He Leadeth Me

Words by JOSEPH H. GILMORE
Music by WILLIAM B. BRADBURY

He lead - eth me! O bless - ed thought! O
And when my task on earth is done, When,

words with heav'n - ly____ com - fort fraught! What - e'er I do, wher -
by Thy grace, the____ vic - t'ry's won, E'en death's cold wave I

e'er I be, Still____ 'tis God's hand____ that____ lead - eth me. He
will not flee, Since____ God through Jor - don____ lead - eth me.

lead - eth me, He lead - eth____ me, By

His own hand__ He__ lead - eth me. His faith - ful fol - l'wer

I would___ be, For by His hand__ He__ lead - eth me.

Shall We Gather At The River

Written & Composed by: Robert Lowry (1826-1899) in 1864
Scripture Reference: Revelation 22:1-2

Robert Lowry was a Baptist minister, and a prominent writer of Sunday-school hymns, although he did not start to write hymns until he was past the age of 40.

This popular revival song was created by Lowry on a hot, sultry day in July of 1864, when he was at the point of exhaustion, after helping out during an epidemic in New York City. He had been busy visiting the sick, and burying members of his Hanson Place Baptist Church where he was pastor. The tune name is "Hanson Place".

Historical Setting For **"SHALL WE GATHER AT THE RIVER"**

Montana Territory was formed out of Idaho Territory in 1864.
Mathew Brady traveled through the war-torn South taking wet-plate pictures and making a photographic record of the Civil War in 1864.
U.S. wheat prices were at four-dollars per bushel in 1864.

Shall We Gather at the River?

Lead, Kindly Light

Words by: John Henry Newman (1801-1890) in 1833
Composed by: John Bacchus Dykes (1823-1876) in 1865
Original Title: "The Pillar Of The Cloud"
Scripture Reference: Exodus 13:21,22 Psalm 32:8 Psalm 43:3

John Newman was born in London, the son of a prosperous banker. and was ordained in 1824 in Oxford, England. Cardinal Newman, co-founder of the Oxford Movement, was an English scholar, and vigorous defender of his religious beliefs. He converted from the Church of England to the Roman Catholic Church in 1845, becoming an ordained priest in 1846. Pope Leo XIII made Newman a cardinal in 1879.

This hymn was written while Newman was traveling aboard a ship from Palermo to Marseilles in 1833. He titled his hymn text "The Pillar of the Cloud", and it was published in 1834 in the "British Magazine". John Newman credited Dykes' tune "Lux Benigna" (meaning "kindly light") with the success of his hymn.

John Dykes was an English clergyman, who wrote nearly 300 hymn tunes. He became a curate at Malton, Yorkshire in 1848, a precentor at Durham Cathedral in 1849, and a vicar of St. Oswald's in 1862. This melody came to Dykes while walking down a crowded London street in the summer of 1865. He published the hymn in 1868 in "Hymns Ancient and Modern...with Appendix". The hymn was sung at the funeral of President McKinley.

Historical Setting For **"LEAD, KINDLY LIGHT"**

The Oxford Movement to restore High Church traditions of the 17th century in the Church of England began in 1833.
Louis Braille invented the Braille system for the blind in 1834.
The estimated Indian population in the U.S. was at 295,000 in 1865, down from 850,000 in 1492.
Decoration Day was celebrated nationally for the first time in 1868.

Lead, Kindly Light

Words by JOHN H. NEWMAN
Music by JOHN B. DYKES

Lead, kind - ly Light, a - mid th'en - cir - cling gloom,
I was not ev - er thus, nor prayed that Thou

Lead Thou me on; The night is dark and I am far from
Shouldst lead me on; I loved to choose and see my path but

home; Lead Thou me on.
now Lead Thou me on.

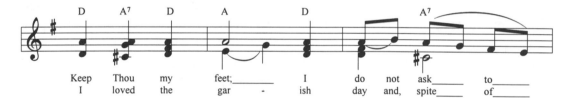

Keep Thou my feet; I do not ask to
I loved the gar - ish day and, spite of

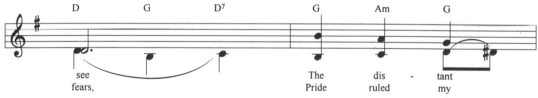

see The dis - tant
fears, Pride ruled my

scene; one step e - nough for me.
will; re - mem - ber not past years.

In The Sweet By And By

Words by: Sanford Fillmore Bennett (1836-1898) in 1867
Composed by: Joseph Philbrick Webster (1819-1875) in 1867
Alternate Title: "There's A Land That Is Fairer Than Day"
Scripture Reference: John 14:2 Isaiah 35:10

The author and composer met in Elkhorn, Wisconsin, where they both had settled to live. They collaborated on several popular songs before writing this hymn in 1867. It first appeared in an 1868 collection of Sunday school songs called "The Signet Ring".

Both words and music for this hymn were completed within a half hour after Webster had made a remark to Bennett that "it will be all right by and by". The hymn was also known as "There's a Land That Is Fairer Than Day".

Sanford Bennett was born in Eden, New York. He became a newspaper editor and pharmacist, as well as an author of many poems. Bennett had served as a 2nd lieutenant in the 40th Wisconsin Volunteers and after the Civil War returned to Elkhorn to open a drugstore. He then took up medicine and worked as a physician beginning in 1874.

Joseph Webster was born in Manchester, New York. He became a talented musician and music teacher, and composer of over 1,000 works. Webster was a sensitive person and frequently suffered from periods of depression. He had settled in Elkhorn before the Civil War and often patronized Bennett's drugstore.

Historical Setting For **"THE SWEET BY AND BY"**

Johann Strauss wrote "The Blue Danube" waltz in 1867.
Russia sold Alaska to the U.S. for $7,200,000 in 1867.
Armour opened it's first meat-packing plant in 1868.
L.M. Alcott wrote "Little Women" in 1868.

In the Sweet By and By

words by SANFORD F. BENNETT
Music by JOSEPH P. WEBSTER

1. There's a land that is fair-er than day, And by

faith we can see it a-far; For the Fa-ther waits o-ver the

way, To pre-pare us a dwell-ing place there. In the

CHORUS (G)

sweet by and by, We shall

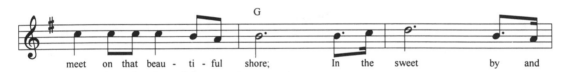

meet on that beau-ti-ful shore; In the sweet by and

by, We shall meet on that beau-ti-ful shore.

2. We shall sing on that beautiful shore
   The melodious songs of the blest,
   And our spirits shall sorrow no more,
   Not a sigh for the blessing of rest.

3. To our bountiful Father above,
   We will offer our tribute of praise,
   For the glorious gift of His love,
   And the blessings that halo low our days.

Tell Me The Old, Old Story

Words by: Arabella Katherine Hankey (1834-1911) in 1866
Composed by: William Howard Doane (1832-1915) in 1867
Scripture Reference: John 10:10 Mark 5:19 Ezekial 3:11

"**K**ate" Hankey was the daughter of a prominent banker in Clapham, a suburb south of London. He was one of a group of evangelical Christians known as the Clapham Sect. They worked for the abolition of slavery in England and were active in promoting missionary endeavors. As a result of these interest within the Hankey family, Kate became interested in religious and social activities.

This children's hymn, as with her other hymn "I Love To Tell The Story", came from a lengthy two-part poem that Hankey had written in 1866, titled "The Story Wanted-The Story Told", about the life of Christ. "Tell Me The Old, Old Story" came from the first half of this 100 verse poem "The Story Wanted".

William Doane composed the music, "Evangel", on a hot summer day while he was riding in a stagecoach in 1867 and included the hymn in his 1870 collection of hymns "Songs of Devotion".

Historical Setting For "TELL ME THE OLD, OLD STORY"

Popular song "When You and I Were Young, Maggie" was published in 1866.
The Christian Science religion was organized by Mary Baker Eddy in 1866.
Austrian composer, Johann Strauss, completed his "Blue Danube" waltz in 1867.
The first bicycle with wire-spoked tension wheels was patented in 1870.
Smith Bros. Cough Drops were patented in 1870.

Tell Me the Old, Old Story

Words by ARABELLA K. HANKEY
Music by WILLIAM H. DOANE

Tell me the old old, story Of unseen things a-
Tell me the story slowly, That I may take it

bove, Of Jesus and His glory, Of Je-
in, That wonderful redemption, God's

sus and His love; Tell me the story simply As
remedy for sin; Tell me the story often, For

to a little child, For I am weak and
I forget so soon; The "early dew" of

weary And helpless and defiled. Tell me the old, old
morning Has passed away at noon.

story, Tell me the old, old story,

Tell me the old, old story Of Jesus and His love.

The Church's One Foundation

Words by: Samuel John Stone (1839-1900) in 1866
Composed by: Samuel Sebastian Wesley (1810-1876) in 1864
Scripture Reference: Ephesians 2:20 Corinthians 3:11

Samuel Stone was born in Whitmore, Staffordshire, England. He was ordained an Anglican clergyman in 1862, and served in that capacity until his death. He was described as the "poor man's pastor" ministering to the poor and underprivileged people in London's East End. He is credited with publishing six collections of hymns.

This hymn was written in 1866 during the "Colenso Controversy" in the Church of England, when the authenticity of the Pentateuch was questioned. It is one of twelve hymns based on the articles of the Apostles' Creed published in Stone's "Lyra Fidelium" in 1866. The tune "Aurelia" was written in 1864 by Samuel Wesley. It had previously been used for the hymn "Jerusalem the Golden", but was matched with Stone's words in 1868.

Samuel Wesley was a grandson of Charles Wesley. Samuel's output of musical compositions was not great, but he did write over 130 hymn tunes, with this one being his best known. He was born in London, England, and served as an organist in five parish churches and four cathedrals.

Historical Setting For "THE CHURCH'S ONE FOUNDATION"

Nevada was admitted as the 36th State in 1864.
The Y.W.C.A. was founded in Boston in 1866.
On Christmas Day 1868, President Andrew Johnson declared amnesty, without exception, to all who had taken a part in the recent rebellion.

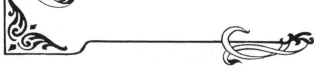

The Church's One Foundation

Words by SAMUEL J. STONE
Music by SAMUEL S. WESLEY

1. The Chur - ch's one Foun - da - tion Is Je - sus Christ her

Lord; She is His new cre - a - tion, By

wa - ter and the word; From heaven He came and

sought her To be His ho - ly Bride; With

His own blood He bought her, And for her life He died.

2. Elect from every nation,
Yet one o'er all the earth,
Her charter of salvation,
One Lord, one faith, one birth;
One holy name she blesses,
Partakes one holy food,
And to one hope she presses,
With every grace endued.

3. 'Mid toil and tribulation,
And tumult of her war,
She waits the consummation
Of peace forever more;
Till with the vision glorious
Her longing eyes are blest,
And the great Church victorious
Shall be the Church at rest.

What A Friend We Have In Jesus

Words by: Joseph Medlicott Scriven (1819-1886) in 1855
Composed by: Charles Crozat Converse (1832-1918) in 1868
Original Title: "Pray Without Ceasing"
Scripture Reference: Matthew 21:22 John 15:13

Joseph Scriven was born in Seapatrick, Ireland, to prosperous parents. The day before Scriven was to have been married, his young bride-to-be was tragically drowned. He never recovered from the shock.

Scriven migrated from Ireland to Canada in 1844, and devoted himself to helping the poor. A second fiancee in Canada died from pneumonia shortly before their scheduled marriage in 1855. His depression in later years may have contributed to his own drowning in 1886.

When asked by a neighbor about the writing of his poem in 1855, Scriven replied that "the Lord and I did it between us". That same neighbor saw to it that his poem, originally title "Pray Without Ceasing", was published in a small collection of poetry called "Hymns and Other Verses".

Charles Converse was born in Warren, Massachusetts. In 1855 he traveled to Leipzig, Germany to study music, then returned to America in 1859, and became a lawyer in 1861. Converse was a pipe-organ enthusiast, and composer of large-scale, serious music. He named the tune for this hymn "Erie" after the Pennsylvania town where he practiced law.

Later he worked with William Bradbury in editing and publishing collections of hymnbooks and Sunday school songbooks. His completed tune for this hymn was written in 1868 and published in 1870 in the "Silver Wings" collection of songs. It was at this time that the hymn was retitled "What A Friend We Have In Jesus" after the first line of the text.

Historical Setting For **"WHAT A FRIEND WE HAVE IN JESUS"**

Florence Nightingale introduced hygienic standards into military hospitals during the Crimean War in 1855.
The game of badminton was created in England in 1868.
Robert E. Lee, Confederate general, died in 1870.

What a Friend We have in Jesus

Words by JOSEPH SCRIVEN
Music by CHARLES C. CONVERSE

What a Friend we have in Je - sus, All our sins and griefs to
Have we tri - als and temp - ta - tions? Is there trou - ble an - y -
Are we weak and heav - y - lad - en, Cum - bered with a load of

bear! What a priv - i - lege to car - ry,
where? We should nev - er be dis - cour - aged;
care? Pre - cious Sav - ior, still our Ref - uge;

Ev - 'ry - thing to God in prayer! O what peace we of - ten
Take it to the Lord in prayer. Can we find a friend so
Take it to the Lord in prayer. Do thy friens de - spise, for -

for - felt, O what need - less pain we bear,
faith - ful, Who will all our sor - rows share?
sake thee? Take it to the Lord in prayer.

All be - cause we do not car - ry, Ev - 'ry - thing to God in prayer!
Je - sus knows our ev - 'ry weak - ness; Take it to the Lord in prayer.
In His arms He'll take and shield thee; Thou wilt find a sol - ace there.

Praise Him, Praise Him

Words by: Fanny Jane Crosby (1820-1915) in 1869
Composed by: Chester G. Allen (1838-1878) in 1869
Original Title: "Praise, Give Thanks"
Scripture Reference: Psalm 146:2

Fanny Crosby is considered the most important writer of gospel hymn texts in American history. She has been referred to as the "queen of gospel music".
This is another of the many favorite gospel hymns by Fanny Crosby.

Chester Allen composed the music for this hymn, which first appeared in a Sunday school hymnal "Bright Jewels", which was published in 1869. The original title was "Praise, Give Thanks". The title was fitting, since this was the same year that "Memorial Day" became a national holiday.

Historical Setting For **"PRAISE HIM, PRAISE HIM"**

Frank Lloyd Wright, American architect, was born in 1869.
The Suez Canal opened in 1869.
General Ulysses S. Grant became the 18th U.S. President in 1869.
The first caricature of "Uncle Sam" with chin whiskers appeared in Harper's Weekly in 1869.

Praise Him! Praise Him!

Words by FANNY K. CROSBY
Music by CHESTER G. ALLEN

Praise Him! Praise Him! Je-sus, our bles-sed Re-deem - er!

Sing O earth His won-der-ful love pro - claim!

Hail Him! Hail Him! High-est arch-an-gels in glo - ry!

Strength and hon - or give to His ho-ly name!

Like a shep-herd, Je-sus will guard His chil - dren.

In His arms He car-ries them all day long;

REFRAIN

Praise Him! Praise Him! Tell of His ex-cel-lent great - ness.

Praise Him! Praise Him! Ev - er in joy - ful song!

Near The Cross

Words by: Fanny Jane Crosby (1820-1915) in 1869
Composed by William Howard Doane (1832-1915) in 1869
Scripture Reference: Colossians 1:19,20 Revelation 22:1-2

Fanny Crosby wrote the words of this hymn to fit an existing tune by William Doane. The hymn was first published in "Bright Jewels" in 1869. Doane was Crosby's principal collaborator over the years. He was a wealthy business man in Cincinnati, as well as a gospel composer and publisher, and left much of his fortune to philanthropic causes.

William Doane published this hymn in 1869. In his early years Doane was in the cotton manufacturing business with his father. After moving to Cincinnati he invented a number of woodworking machines while he was the head of a large woodworking plant.

Doane began writing hymn tunes in 1862 while recovering from a serious illness. He compiled over 40 songbooks and wrote some 2,300 songs, ballads, and cantatas.

Historical Setting For "NEAR THE CROSS"

Campbell Soup Co., H.J. Heinz Co., and Welch's Grape all had their beginnings in 1869. Purdue University was founded in 1869.

Near the Cross

Words by FANNY J. CROSBY
Music by WILLIAM H. DOANE

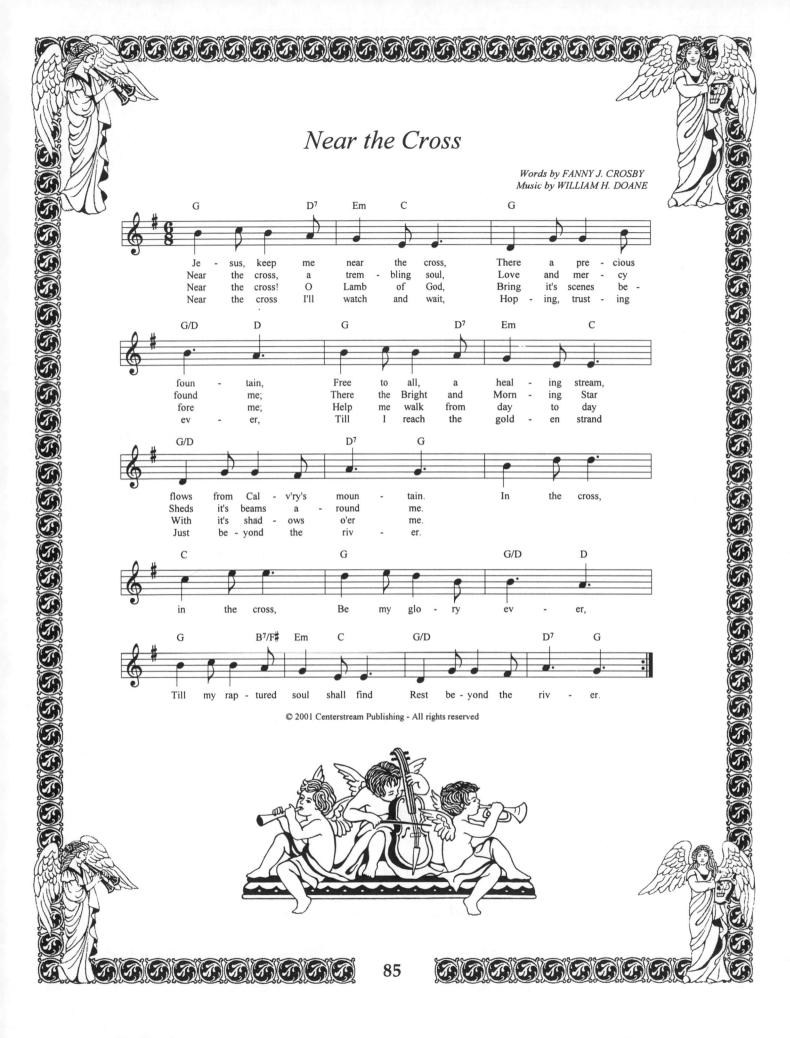

Je - sus, keep me near the cross, There a pre - cious
Near the cross, a trem - bling soul, Love and mer - cy
Near the cross! O Lamb of God, Bring it's scenes be -
Near the cross I'll watch and wait, Hop - ing, trust - ing

foun - tain, Free to all, a heal - ing stream,
found me; There the Bright and Morn - ing Star
fore me; Help me walk from day to day
ev - er, Till I reach the gold - en strand

flows from Cal - v'ry's moun - tain. In the cross,
Sheds it's beams a - round me.
With it's shad - ows o'er me.
Just be - yond the riv - er.

in the cross, Be my glo - ry ev - er,

Till my rap - tured soul shall find Rest be - yond the riv - er.

Christ For The World We Sing

Words by: Samuel Wolcott (1813-1886) in 1869
Composed by Felice de Giardini (1716-1796) in 1769
Scripture Reference: Matthew 28:19,20   Acts 10:35

Samuel Wolcott was an American Congregational clergyman and missionary. He was a missionary in Syria from 1840 to 1842, and later pastored churches in Rhode Island, Illinois, and Ohio.

Wolcott wrote more than 200 hymns after the age of 56. He wrote this hymn in 1869 while walking through the streets after coming home from a Y.M.C.A. evangelistic service in Ohio where a motto there "Christ For the World and The World for Christ" inspired Wolcott to write the song. At the time Wolcott was the minister at Plymouth Congregational Church in Cleveland, Ohio. The hymn was first published in William Doane's 1870 "Songs of Devotion".

Felice de Giardini was born in Turin, Italy where he was trained as a chorister in Milan Cathedral. He moved to London, where he became a popular violinist beginning in 1750. Later, he moved to Moscow where he spent the remainder of his life. Poverty and distress over the loss of his former fame hastened his death in 1796.

The tune "Italian Hymn" composed in 1769 by Giardini for the hymn "Come, Thou Almighty King" was later to be used for this hymn. The tune made it's first appearance in the "Lock Collection" in 1769.

Historical Setting For **"CHRIST FOR THE WORLD WE SING"**

James Cook discovered Australia in 1769.
Napoleon Bonaparte was born in 1769.
Famous Ottawa chief, Pontiac, was murdered in 1769.
Pope Pius IX declared abortion of any kind an excommunicatory sin in 1869.
The first U.S. plow with a moldboard entirely of chilled steel was patented by James Oliver in 1869.
The Universities of St. John's, Syracuse, Ohio State, Cincinnati and Texas Christian were founded in 1870.
Only 2% of Americans 17 years and older are high school graduates in 1870.

Christ for the World! We Sing
Italian Hymn

Words by SAMUEL WOLCOTT
Music by FELICE de GIARDINI

1. Christ for the world!___ we sing; The world to
2. Christ for the world!___ we sing; The world to
3. Christ for the world!___ we sing; The world to
4. Christ for the world!___ we sing; The world to

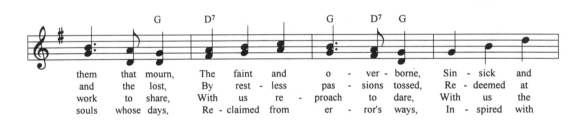

Christ_____ we bring, With lov - ing zeal; The poor and
Christ_____ we bring, With fer - vent prayer; The way - ward
Christ_____ we bring, With one ac - cord; With us the
Christ_____ we bring, With joy - ful song; The new - born

them that mourn, The faint and o - ver - borne, Sin - sick and
and the lost, By rest - less pas - sions tossed, Re - deemed at
work to share, With us re - proach to dare, With us the
souls whose days, Re - claimed from er - ror's ways, In - spired with

sor - row - worn, Whom Christ doth heal. A - men.
count - less cost, From dark des - pair.
cross to bear, For Christ our Lord.
hope and praise, To Christ be - long.

More Love To Thee

Words by: Elizabeth Payson Prentiss (1818-1878) in 1856
Composed by: William Howard Doane (1832-1915) 1870
Scripture Reference: Philippians 1:9-11 John 15:9 Ephesians 6:24

Elizabeth Prentiss was born in Portland, Maine, and married in 1845. During her life she was a successful writer of children's books, popular stories, prose and poetry. She was also a teacher in Maine, Massachusetts and Virginia.

Throughout her life she was a near invalid with a frail body. This hymn was written in 1856, shortly after the death of two of her children in the 1856 epidemic that swept New York. She never showed the poem to anyone for the next 13 years.

In 1869 she showed the poem to her husband, George Prentiss, and he encouraged her to publish the poem in a leaflet to be distributed among friends that year. One of the leaflets came to the attention of William Doane.

Doane was a successful Cincinnati businessman whose hobby was writing gospel-song tunes (over 2,200 all together). He was Fanny Crosby's principal collaborator in writing Gospel music. He included this hymn in his hymnal "Songs of Devotion", published in 1870. The tune name is titled "More Love To Thee".

Historical Setting For "MORE LOVE TO THEE"

"Big Ben", the 13.5 ton bell at the British Houses of Parliament, was cast at Whitechapel Bell Foundry in 1856.

The nation was connected by rail at Promontory Point, Utah in 1869 with the joining of the Union Pacific and Central Pacific railroads.

The University of Nebraska was founded in Lincoln in 1869.

DNA was discovered in 1870 by chemistry student Friederich Miescher.

More Love to Thee

Words by ELIZABERTH P. PRENTISS
Music by WILLIAM H. DOANE

1. More love to Thee, O Christ, More love to
2. Once earth - ly joy I craved, Sought peace and
3. Then shall my lat - est breath Whis - per Thy

Thee! Hear Thou the prayer I make
rest; Now Thee a - lone I seek,
praise; This be the part - ing cry

On bend - ed knee; This is my
Give what is best; This all my
My heart shall raise; This still it's

ear - nest plea: More love, O Christ, to Thee,
prayer shall be:
prayer shall be:

More love to Thee, More love to Thee!

Pass Me Not, O Gentle Saviour

Words by: Fanny Jane Crosby (1820-1915) in 1868
Composed by: William Howard Doane (1832-1915) in 1870
Scripture Reference: Psalm 69:16   Genesis 18:3

Fanny Crosby was blind from the sixth week of her life, due to a physician's mistake. As a young woman she taught at the New York School for the Blind. She was a lifelong friend of Grover Cleveland. More than 500 of her 8,000 hymns were published, and many were signed Fanny C. Van Alstyne, after she had married Alexander Van Alstyne at age 38.

She wrote this hymn text in 1868. William Doane composed and published the hymn in his 1870 collection of hymns "Songs of Devotion".

Historical Setting For **"PASS ME NOT, O GENTLE SAVIOUR"**

The famous King ranch in Texas was now at 300,000 acres in 1868.
Memorial Day was observed for the first time in 1868 to commemorate the Union dead of the Civil War.
Cattle drives up the Chisholm Trail from San Antonio to Abilene, Kansas, began on a big scale in 1870.
Kansas City's population jumped from 3,500 in 1865 to 32,260 in 1870.

Pass Me Not, O Gentle Savior

Words by FANNY CROSBY
Music by WILLIAM H. DOANE

Pass me not, O gen-tle Sav - ior; Hear my hum-ble
Let me at the throne of mer - cy Find a sweet re-
Trust - ing on - ly in Thy mer - it, Would I seek Thy
Thou, the spring of all my com - fort, More than life to

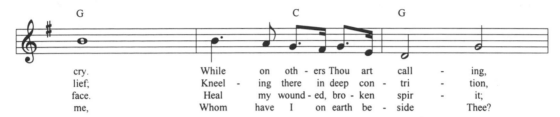

cry. While on oth-ers Thou art call - ing,
lief; Kneel - ing there in deep con - tri - tion,
face. Heal my wound-ed, bro-ken spir - it;
me, Whom have I on earth be - side Thee?

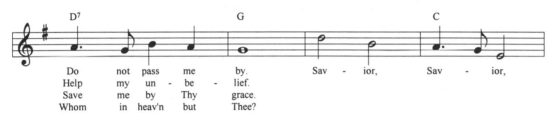

Do not pass me by. Sav - ior, Sav - ior,
Help my un - be - lief.
Save me by Thy grace.
Whom in heav'n but Thee?

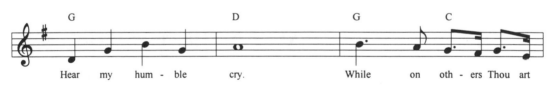

Hear my hum-ble cry. While on oth-ers Thou art

call - ing, Do not pass me by.

Rescue The Perishing

Words by: Fanny Jane Crosby (1820-1915) in 1869
Composed by: William Howard Doane (1832-1915) in 1870
Scripture Reference: Isaiah 61:1 Jude 1:23

Fanny Crosby was born in Putnam county, New York. Her given name was Frances Jane Crosby, but she normally went by Fanny J. Blinded through a physician's negligence at the age of six weeks, she entered the New York City Institution for the Blind around 1835, and taught there from 1847 to 1858. In 1858, she married a blind musician, Alexander Van Alstyne. Crosby wrote this hymn text in 1869.

William Doane was born in Preston, Connecticut. He was a prosperous factory president who was interested in music only as an avocation. Doane wrote and published more than 2,000 gospel songs and tunes. This hymn was published in his 1870 collection "Songs of Devotion". Doane suggested the hymn title "Rescue the Perishing".

Historical Setting For **"RESCUE THE PERISHING"**

The Great Wall Street Panic known as "Black Friday" took place on September 24, 1869.
William F. Cody first became known as "Buffalo Bill" in 1869.
Dwight L. Moody and Ira D. Sankey teamed up to spread the Gospel by word and song in 1870.
Roller skating was gaining popularity in the U.S. in 1870.

Rescue the Perishing

Words by FANNY J. CROSBY
Music by WILLIAM H. DOANE

Res - cue the per - ish - ing, Care for the dy - ing, Snatch them in pi - ty from
Res - cue the per - ish - ing; Du - ty de - mands it, Strength for thy la - bor the

sin and the grave; Weep o'er the err - ing one, Lift up the fall - en,
Lord will pro - vide; Back to the nar - row way Pa - tient - ly win them,

Tell them of Je - sus the might - y to save. Res - cue the per - ish - ing,
Tell the poor wan - d'rer a Sav - iour has died.

Care for the dy - ing; Je - sus is mer - ci - ful, Je - sus will save.

Onward Christian Soldiers

Words by: Sabine Baring-Gould (1834-1924) in 1865
Composed by: Arthur Seymour Sullivan (1842-1900) in 1871
Original Title: "Hymn For Procession With Cross & Banners"
Scripture Reference: Matthew 16:18   Ephesians 6:13

Sabine Baring-Gould was born in Exeter, England. He became an Anglican clergyman in 1857 at the Yorkshire village of Horbury. It was there that he wrote this hymn in 1864 in his usual custom of writing while standing at a writing table. The British novelist wrote 85 books on history, biography, poetry, fiction, travel, religion, mythology, folklore, etc.   Baring-Gould is considered a pioneer in the collection of folk songs. He wrote this hymn in a single night for a children's parade, during the religious holiday of Whitsunday and it was first sung to a melody by Haydn. The original title was "Hymn for Procession with Cross and Banners", and was published in a religious magazine called "Church Times" in 1865.

Sir Arthur Sullivan was born at Bolwell Terrace, England, and composed the tune "St. Gertrude" for this hymn. He was an organist, professor of composition, and conductor of choral concerts and music festivals. Sullivan's musical setting is not the original, but has become universally accepted.   The original music was a slow movement from a Haydn symphony. Sullivan (of Gilbert and Sullivan comic opera fame) wrote the melody in 1871 and it was published that year in "Musical Times" in London. It was published in his own "The Church Hymnary" in 1872.

Historical Setting For **"ONWARD CHRISTIAN SOLDIERS"**

Clara Barton was placed in charge of a government-sponsored search for missing soldiers of the Civil War in 1865.
Interest in baseball surged after the Civil War ended in 1865.
Baseball became a professional sport in the U.S. in 1871.
P.T. Barnum organized his circus "The Greatest Show On Earth" in 1871.
The first penny postcards in the U.S. were issued in 1873.

Onward, Christian Soldiers

Words by SABINE BARING-GOULD
Mucis by ARTHUR S. SULLIVAN

Let The Lower Lights Be Burning

Written & Composed by: Philip Paul Bliss (1838-1876) in 1871
Scripture Reference: Matthew 5:16 Luke 12:35

This song first appeared in Bliss' earliest songbook "The Charm" in 1871. It also came out in his 1874 "Gospel Songs". Bliss wrote the song after listening to a sermon by Dwight L. Moody that included a story about the lower lights along the shore of Lake Erie, near Cleveland.

Bliss was born in a log cabin, left home at age eleven to work on farms and in lumber camps. He became a Christian at age twelve, married at 21, and became a traveling music teacher when he was 22. He was equally skilled at writing both words and music to Christian songs.

Bliss first met Dwight L. Moody in Chicago in 1869, and soon joined Moody and Ira Sankey, in their evangelistic campaign. Bliss died in a train accident in Ohio, during the Christmas season of 1876.

Historical Setting For "LET THE LOWER LIGHTS BE BURNING"

Stanley found Livingstone in Africa in 1871.
The U.S. population was at 39 million in 1871.
The Great Chicago Fire occurred in 1871.
The National Rifle Association was formed in 1871.

Let the Lower Lights Be Burning

by PHILIP P. BLISS

1. Bright - ly beams our Fa - ther's mer - cy, From His
2. Dark the night of sin has set - tled, Loud the

light - house ev - er - more. But to us, He gives the
an - gry bill - ows roar. Ea - ger eyes are watch - ing,

keep - ing of the lights a - long the shore. Let the
long - ing for the lights a - long the shore.

low - er lights be burn - ing, Send a gleam a - cross the

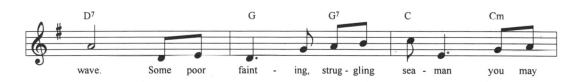

wave. Some poor faint - ing, strug - gling sea - man you may

res - cue, you may save. Dark the save.

Faith Of Our Fathers

Words by: Frederick William Faber (1814-1863) in 1849
Composed by: Henri Frederick Hemy (1818-1888) in 1864
Adapted by James George Walton (1821-1905) in 1871
Scripture Reference: Jude 3 Hebrews 11:1-2

Frederick Faber was born in Yorkshire, England. He was ordained an Anglican priest in 1837, then later, became an ardent follower of the Oxford Movement, and converted to the Roman Catholic faith in 1846, at which time he took the name Wilfred, and founded a religious community in Birmingham England.

Faber wrote over 150 hymns promoting the history and teachings of the Catholic church. This hymn text first appeared in 1849 in the author's collection, "Jesus and Mary; or Catholic Hymns for Singing and Reading".

Henri Hemy was born at Newcastle-upon-Tyne, England. He was a respected composer, and an English Catholic church organist, a professor of music, and teacher of piano and singing. His best known hymn tune is "St. Catherine" for "Faith of Our Fathers", which first appeared in his collection "Crown of Jesus Music" in 1864.

James Walton added the refrain and adapted the tune by Hemy in 1871 for his collection "Plain Song Music for the Holy Communion Office", published in 1874.

Historical Setting For **"FAITH OF OUR FATHERS"**

General Zachary Taylor, "Old Rough and Ready", was inaugurated as the 12th U.S. President in 1849.
The California Gold Rush had many prospectors heading west in 1849.
The Post Office introduced money orders in 1864.
Railroad mail delivery began in 1864.
The song "Reuben and Rachel" was published in 1871.
The 1st American zoo was established in Philadelphia in 1874.

Faith of Our Fathers

Words by FREDRICK W. FABER
Music by HENRI F. HEMY

2. Our fathers, chained in prisons dark,
   Were still in heart and conscience free,
   And blest would be their children's fate,
   Tho they, like them, should die for thee:
   Faith of our fathers, holy faith,
   We will be true to thee till death.

3. Faith of our fathers, we will love
   Both friend and foe in all our strife,
   And preach thee, too, as love knows how
   By kindly words and virtuous life:
   Faith of our fathers, holy faith,
   We will be true to thee till death.

I Need Thee Every Hour

Words by: Annie Sherwood Hawks (1835-1918) in 1872
Composed by: Robert Lowry (1826-1899) in 1872
Scripture Reference: Psalm 86:7

Annie Hawks was born in Hoosick, New York. She started writing poetry for newspapers at the young age of fourteen. She married Charles Hawks at age 24 and this hymn was hastily written by Hawks while busily performing her household duties as a housewife and mother on a bright June morning in 1872.

Hawks recalled "Suddenly, I became filled with a sense of nearness to the master, and I began to wonder how anyone could ever live without him, either in joy or pain." She was inspired to write hymns by Robert Lowry after moving to Brooklyn, and eventually penned more than 400.

Robert Lowry was the pastor at Hanson Place Baptist Church in Brooklyn when he first met Annie Hawks. Lowry added the hymn's refrain, as well as composed the tune "Need". He introduced the song at the National Baptist Sunday School Convention in Cincinnati in November of 1872. The hymn was first published by Lowry in 1873 in Lowry's "Royal Diadem" hymn book.

Lowry published such other Gospel song collections as "Bright Jewels" in 1869, "Pure Gold for the Sunday School" in 1871, and "Good as Gold".

Historical Setting For "I NEED THEE EVERY HOUR"

Jules Verne wrote "Around the World in 80 Days" in 1872.
U.S. President Calvin Coolidge was born in 1872.
Arbor Day was first observed in 1872, in Nebraska.
Jules Verne published the fiction adventure story "Twenty Thousand Leagues Under The Sea in 1873.

I Need Thee Every Hour

Words by ANNIE S. HAWKS
Music by ROBERT LOWRY

Blessed Assurance

Words by: Fanny Jane Crosby (1820-1915) in 1873
Composed by: Phoebe Palmer Knapp (1839-1908) in 1873
Scripture Reference: Hebrews 10:22,23 John 6:47

Fanny Crosby wrote more than 8,000 song texts after she began writing gospel songs in the 1860's. She lost her sight at age six weeks and was blind the rest of her life.

The verses for this hymn were written within two hours after Crosby heard Phoebe Knapp play the tune in 1873. This speed in writing hymns was nothing unusual for this gifted lady who wrote "Safe in the Arms of Jesus" in about 15 minutes and could compose as many as six or seven hymns in one day.

Phoebe Knapp attended the same Methodist church in New York City as Fanny Crosby. She was married to the founder of the Metropolitan Life Insurance Co., Joseph Knapp, and published more than 500 hymn tunes. The tune for this hymn is titled "Blessed Assurance", composed in 1873.

Historical Setting For **"BLESSED ASSURANCE"**

The lyrics to "Home On The Range" were published in 1873.
Barbed wire production had its beginning in 1873.

Blessed Assurance

Lyrics by FANNY CROSBY and VAN ALSTYNE
Music by PHOEBE P. KNAPP

I Gave My Life For Thee

Words by: Frances Ridley Havergal (1836-1879) in 1858
Composed by: Philip Paul Bliss (1838-1876) in 1873
Original Title: "Thy Life Was Given For Me"
Scripture Reference: 2 Corinthians 5:15   Mark 10:45

Frances Havergal was nicknamed "Little Quicksilver" by her father, because she learned quickly and enjoyed every new discovery to the fullest. Her bright, cheerful disposition endeared her to all who knew her. Educated in England and Germany, she became proficient in the Italian, French, German, Latin, Greek, and Hebrew languages.

Frances Havergal wrote these words in 1858 after viewing a deeply moving painting of Christ, "Ecce Homo", in Dusseldorf, Germany. However, she felt the poetry was so poor that she tossed the poem in a stove, but it somehow escaped the flames and was salvaged by her father, who encouraged her to preserve the verses. It was printed in a leaflet in 1859 and the following year was included in an issue of "Good Words", a religious periodical.

Philip Bliss composed the tune "Kenosis" for this hymn in 1873 and it was published in his "Sunshine for Sunday Schools" that same year. It was dedicated to the Railroad Chapel Sunday School in Chicago.

Historical Setting For "I GAVE MY LIFE FOR THEE"

The "Wedding March" by Felix Mendelssohn gained popularity in 1858 when it was used in a British royal wedding.
The first typewriter to be placed on the market was by Sholes and Glidden in 1873.
The Royal Canadian Mounted Police were organized in 1873.

I Gave My Life for Thee

Words by FRANCES R. HAVERGAL
Music by PHILIP P. BLISS

1. I gave My life for thee, My pre - cious blood I
2. My Fa - ther's house of light, My glo - ry cir - cled
3. I suf - fered much for thee, More that thy tongue can
4. And I have brought to thee, Down from My home a -

shed,_____ That thou might'st ran - somed be,_____ And
throne,_____ I left for earth - ly night,_____ For
tell,_____ Of bit - t'rest ag - o - ny,_____ To
bove,_____ Sal - va - tion full and free,_____ My

quick - ened from the dead;_____ I gave, I gave My
wan - d'rings sad and lone;_____ I left, I left it
res - cue thee from hell;_____ I've borne, I've borne it
par - don and My love;_____ I bring, I bring rich

life for thee, What hast thou giv'n for Me?_____
all for thee, Hast thou left aught for Me?_____
all for thee, What hast thou borne for Me?_____
gifts to thee, What hast thou brought to Me?_____

When Morning Gilds The Skies

Author Unknown
German Folk Song from 1828
English translation by: Edward Caswall (1814-1878) in 1854
Composed by: Joseph Barnby (1838-1896) in 1868
Original Title: "A Christian Greeting"
Scripture Reference: Job 1:21
Revelation 4:11 & Psalm 54:6

Ed Caswall was born in Hampshire, England. He was an English clergyman, ordained in 1839, who left the Anglican Church in 1846 to become a Roman Catholic priest in 1847.

He published many hymns with mostly Roman Catholic doctrinal content. The German words to this hymn first appeared in the "Katholisches Gesangbuch" in 1828. Around 1850, Caswall published "Lyra Catholica", a collection of 197 English translations of Latin hymns. He translated this hymn in 1854.

Joseph Barnby was born in York, England. He was a well-known English church organist, composer, editor and choral director who wrote 246 hymns (published after his death in 1897), and edited five hymn books. His tune name for this German folk hymn is "Laudes Domini", composed in 1868 and first published in the appendix to "Hymns Ancient & Modern" that same year. It was first sung at St. Paul's Catherdral in London. Copies were distributed to the congregation in leaflet form and Barnby led the choir and congregation in the singing of the new hymn and tune. The hymn as we know it today was first published in "Hymns and Poems" in 1873. Barnby was knighted in 1892.

Historical Setting For "WHEN MORNING GILDS THE SKIES"

Noah Webster published his first dictionary in 1828.
The U.S. acquired parts of New Mexico and Arizona in 1854.
U.S. President Andrew Johnson was impeached in 1868.
The Fourteenth Amendment to the Constitution was adopted in 1868.
It granted citizenship to all those born or naturalized in the U.S.

When Morning Gilds the Skies

Author unknown
English translation by EDWARD CASWALL
Music by JOSEPH BARNBY
German folk song

When morn - ing gilds the skies,_____ My
In heav'n's e - ter - nal bliss_____ The

heart a - wak - ing cries, "May
love - liest strain is this, "May

Je - sus Christ___ be praised!" A - like at work and
Je - sus Christ___ be praised!" The pow'rs of dark - ness

pray'r To Je - sus I re - pair. "May
fear, When this sweet chant they hear: "May

Je - sus Christ be_____ praised!"
Je - sus Christ be_____ praised!"

It Is Well With My Soul

Words by: Horatio Gates Spafford (1828-1888) in 1873
Composed by: Philip Paul Bliss (1838-1876) in 1873
Scripture Reference: Psalm 146:1

Horatio Spafford lived a peaceful life until 1871. In that year, the great Chicago fire, wiped out his family's extensive real estate investments. Then in 1873, Spafford's four daughters, Anna, Maggie, Bessie and Tanetta, were all drowned in the accidental sinking of the ship "S.S. Ville du Havre". Only his wife, Anna, was saved from the icy waters and Spafford sailed to England to be with his grieving wife.

The Spafford's close friend, Evangelist Dwight L. Moody, joined them and later noted that, though they were experiencing deep sorrow, the Spaffords never lost their abiding faith in God. They attested to this with their affirmation to Moody, "It is well. The will of God be done." Spafford wrote this hymn in the aftermath of this tragedy.

Spafford's friend, Philip Bliss, composed the music, "Ville de Havre", to this hymn in 1873. It was first published in Bliss' 1876 hymnal "Gospel Hymns No. Two". In most cases, Bliss wrote both the words and music for his hymns.

Historical Setting For "IT IS WELL WITH MY SOUL"

One cent post cards were placed on sale by the Post Office in 1873.
The first cable-car system in the U.S. was introduced in San Francisco in 1873.
Oscar Hammerstein entered show business in 1876.
John Hopkins University was founded in Baltimore in 1876.

It is Well with My Soul

Words by HORATIO G. SPAFFORD
Music by PHILIP P. BLISS

When peace like a riv - er at -
Though Sa - tan should buf - fet, though
My sin, O, the bliss of this
And Lord, haste the day when the

tend - eth my way, When sor - rows like
tri - als should come, Let this blest as
glo - ri - ous thought; My sin, not in
faith shall be sight, The clouds be rolled

sea bil - lows roll; What - ev - er my
sur - ance con - trol, That Christ hath re -
part, but the whole, Is nailed to the
back as a scroll; The trump shall re -

lot, Thou hast taught me to say "It is
gard - ed my help - less es - tate, And hath
cross and I bear it no more. Praise the
sound and the Lord shall de - scend, "E - ven

well, it is well with my soul." It is
shed His own blood for my soul.
Lord, praise the Lord, O my soul!
so" it is well with my soul.

well_____ with my soul,_____ It is

well, It is well with my soul.

Crown Him With Many Crowns

Words by: Matthew Bridges (1800-1894) in 1851
3rd Verse by Godfrey Thring (1823-1903) in 1874
Composed by: George Job Elvey (1816-1893) in 1868
Original Title: "Third Sorrowful Mystery, Song of the Seraphs"
Scripture Reference: Revelation 19:12

This hymn was written in 1851 and first appeared in 1852 in Bridge's "The Passion of Jesus". The first, second and fourth verses of the current hymn were written by Bridges.

Bridges was born in Malden, Essex, England. He was raised in the Anglican Church, but came under the influence of the Oxford Movement, and joined the Roman Catholic Church in 1848. His works include volumes of poetry, sermons and history, with his earliest poems appearing in 1825.

The third verse was written by Thring 23 years after the verses by Bridges, and the completed hymn appeared in "Hymns and Sacred Lyrics" in 1874. Thring was born in Alford, England. He was ordained an Anglican clergyman in 1846.

George Elvey, a noted English organist, wrote the tune "Diademata" (Greek word for crowns) in 1868. It appeared in the Appendix of "Hymns Ancient and Modern" that same year. Elvey was born in Canterbury, England. He served as organist of the St. George's Chapel in Windsor for 47 years from 1835 to 1882. He was knighted by Queen Victoria in 1871.

Historical Setting For **"CROWN HIM WITH MANY THORNS"**

Popular songs "Old Folks At Home" and "Wait For The Wagon" were published in 1851.
The phrase "Go West, young man" was popularized in 1851.
Surveys began of the Grand Canyon and Colorado River in 1868.
Tchaikovsky debuted his "Symphony No. 1" in 1868.
The U.S. was in the midst of a fifteen year series of military conflicts with the Apache Indians in 1874.
The first Hutterite immigrants came to America in 1874.

Crown Him with Many Crowns

Words by MATTHEW BRIDGES and GODFREY THRING
Music by GEORGE J. ILVEY

1. Crown Him with man - y crowns, the Lamb up - on His
2. Crown Him the Lord of years, the Po - ten - tate of

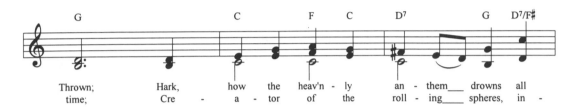

Thrown; Hark, how the heav'n - ly an - them___ drowns all
time; Cre - a - tor of the roll - ing___ spheres, in -

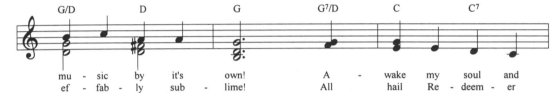

mu - sic by it's own! A - wake my soul and
ef - fab - ly sub - lime! All hail Re - deem - er

sing of Him who died for Thee, And
hail! For Thou hast died for me, Thy

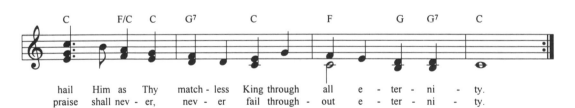

hail Him as Thy match - less King through all e - ter - ni - ty.
praise shall nev - er, nev - er fail through - out e - ter - ni - ty.

Christ Arose

Written & Composed by Robert Lowry (1826-1899) in 1874
Scripture Reference: Romans 6:8,9 Luke 24:6

Perhaps the most beloved of Easter hymns is "Christ Arose". Robert Lowry was born in Philadelphia, Pa. He accepted Christ at the age of 17. He was a professor of literature, pastored several Baptist churches, and became the music editor of the Biglow Publishing Co. It is said that the quality of Lowry's numerous publications did much to improve the cause of sacred music in America.

Lowry wrote this hymn during the Easter season of 1874, and it was published the next year in the collection "Brightest and Best" by William Doane and Robert Lowry.

Historical Setting For **"CHRIST AROSE"**

The first bridge over the Mississippi opened at St. Louis in 1874.
Madison Square Garden opened in 1874.
The first American made Christmas cards appeared in 1875.
Vaseline petroleum jelly was introduced in 1875.

Christ Arose

Words and Music by
ROBERT LOWRY

Wonderful Words Of Life

Written & Composed by: Philip Paul Bliss (1838-1876) in 1874
Scripture Reference: John 6:63 Phillipians 2:15-16

Philip Bliss wrote "Wonderful Words Of Life" in 1874 for the first issue of a Sunday school paper titled "Words Of Life".

Bliss was born in a log cabin in Clearfield, Pennsylvania. He was converted at the age of twelve and joined a Baptist church near Elk Run, Pennsylvania. His musical talents were evident at an early age. As a young man he was employed by musician, George F. Root.

With his wife, his horse named Fanny, and a reed organ, he began traveling and teaching music professionally in 1860, and then began publishing music in 1865. He published four collections of his work from 1871 to 1874. At the urging of Dwight Moody, he put his musical talents to work in evangelism meetings beginning in 1874.

In a railway accident at Ashtabula, Ohio, in December 1876, a cast-iron bridge gave way plunging seven cars into an icy riverbed. Bliss managed to survive the fall and the fire that broke out in the wreckage by escaping through a window, but he died when he went back to try and rescue his wife.

Historical Setting For **"WONDERFUL WORDS OF LIFE"**

The ice cream soda was invented in 1874 by Robert Green.
Margarine was introduced to the United States in 1874.
The first Remington typewriters were introduced by Remington & Sons Fire Arms Co. in 1874.
Levi Strauss blue jeans began using copper rivets in 1874.

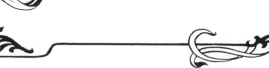

Wonderful Words of Life

Words and Music by PHILIP P. BLISS

1. Sing them o - ver a - gain to me, Won - der - ful words of
2. Christ, the bless - ed One, gives to all, Won - der - ful words of
3. Sweet - ly ech - o the gos - pel call, Won - der - ful words of

Life; Let me more of their beau - ty see,
Life; Sin - ner, list to the lov - ing call,
Life; Of - fer par - don and peace to all,

Won - der - ful words of Life; Words of life and beau - ty,
Won - der - ful words of Life; All so free - ly giv - en,
Won - der - ful words of Life; Je - sus, on - ly Sav - iour,

Teach me faith and du - ty: Beau - ti - ful words,
Woo - ing us to heav - en:
Sanc - ti - fy for - ev - er:

won - der - ful words, Won - der - ful words of Life. Life.

Take My Life And Let It Be

Words by: Frances Ridley Havergal (1836-1879) in 1874
Composed by: Henry Abraham Cesar Malan (1787-1864) in 1823
Scripture Reference: Ephesians 6:24   Romans 12:1 I Corinthians 6:19

Frances Havergal was born in Astley, England. At the age of four she started reading and memorizing the Bible.

Havergal became an English poet and devotional writer. She has been called "The Consecration Poet". Her father inspired her to write, because he too was an accomplished hymn writer. She is credited with writing 50 hymns and 200 poems. She was also a talented pianist and singer. This hymn text was written at Areley House on February 4, 1874 after Havergal had helped convert some people to Christianity. It first appeared in print in her "Loyal Responses" in 1878.

Henry Malan was born in Geneva, Switzerland, and became a Swiss Reformed pastor. He wrote over 1,000 hymns and made several missionary journeys to Germany, France, the Netherlands, and Scotland. He's compared with Isaac Watts   for promoting the general recognition of hymns in public worship, especially in France. His tune name used with this hymn is "Hendon", named after a high hill located near London. Malan composed the tune in 1823.

Historical Setting For **"TAKE MY LIFE AND LET IT BE"**

President Monroe announced his "Monroe Doctrine" in 1823.
Clement Clarke Moore wrote "A Visit from St. Nicholas" in 1823.
The game of tennis was introduced to America in 1874.
Herbert Hoover and Winston Churchill were born in 1874.

Take My Life and Let It Be

Words by FRANCIS R. HAVERGAL
Music by HENRY A.C. MALAN

Take my life____ and____ let it be

con - se - cra - ted,____ Lord to____ Thee.

Take my hands and___ let them move____ at the im - pulse

of___ Thy___ love,___ at the im - pulse___ of Thy love.

The Ninety And Nine

Words by: Elizabeth Cecilia Clephane (1830-1869)
Composed by: Ira David Sankey (1840-1908) in 1874
Scripture Reference: Luke 15:7

Elizabeth Clephane was born in Edinburgh, Scotland, daughter of a sheriff, but was raised an orphan after her fathers death. Clephane became a poet while living in Melrose.

She had a frail body and was in poor health most of her life, but dedicated her limited resources to benefit the poor in her community. Her nickname was "Sunbeam" among the sick and dying in her area. She wrote eight hymns and all of them were published posthumously in a monthly magazine "The Family Treasury".

This poem was published in a Glasgow paper in 1874, but the exact year it was written is unknown, although it was written not long before her death. The text is based on a Scripture parable from Luke 15:3-7. The poem attracted the attention of Ira Sankey, who cut the words from the paper he was reading, with a tune already taking form in his mind.

Ira Sankey was born in Lawrence County, Pa. After serving in the Union Army during the Civil War, he became a clerk for the Internal Revenue Service. Beginning in 1870, he was closely associated with the revival campaigns of D.L. Moody. Sankey composed the tune for this hymn the same year the text was published in 1874.

Historical Setting For "THE NINETY AND NINE"

The first public zoo in the U.S. opened in 1874.
The first practical barbed wire fencing was invented in 1874.

The Ninety and Nine

Words by ELIZBETH C. CLEPHANE
Music by IRA D. SANKEY

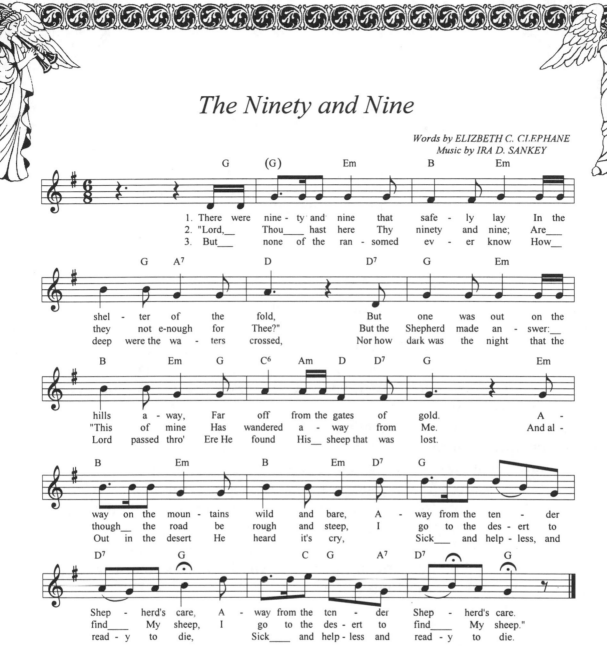

1. There were nine-ty and nine that safe-ly lay In the shel-ter of the fold, But one was out on the hills a-way, Far off from the gates of gold. A-way on the moun-tains wild and bare, A-way from the ten-der Shep-herd's care, A-way from the ten-der Shep-herd's care.

2. "Lord, Thou hast here Thy ninety and nine; Are they not e-nough for Thee?" But the Shepherd made an-swer: "This of mine Has wandered a-way from Me. And al-though the road be rough and steep, I go to the des-ert to find My sheep, I go to the des-ert to find My sheep."

3. But none of the ran-somed ev-er know How deep were the wa-ters crossed, Nor how dark was the night that the Lord passed thro' Ere He found His sheep that was lost. Out in the desert He heard it's cry, Sick and help-less, and read-y to die, Sick and help-less and read-y to die.

4. "Lord, whence are those blood drops all the way
That mark out the mountain's track?"
"They were shed for one who had gone astray
Ere the shepherd could bring him back."
"Lord, whence are Thy hands so rent and torn?"
"They're pierced tonight by many a thorn.
They're pierced tonight by many a thorn."

5. But all thro' the mountains, thunder riv'n,
And up from the rocky steep,
There arose a glad cry to the gate of heav'n,
"Rejoice! I have found my sheep!"
And the angels echoed around the throne,
"Rejoice, for the Lord brings back His own!
Rejoice, for the Lord brings back His own."

I Love To Tell The Story

Words by: Arabella Katherine Hankey (1834-1911) in 1866
Composed by: William Gustavus Fischer (1835-1912) in 1869
Scripture Reference: Psalm 66:16
Proverbs 11:30   Psalm 145:5

Katherine Hankey was born into wealth in London, and used her resources to teach the Bible to poor working girls and to assist evangelical groups. She taught Sunday school and organized Bible study classes. Miss Hankey was a successful writer on religious subjects inspired by her experiences as a Sunday School teacher. She was a member of the "Clapham Sect" dedicated to evangelistic enterprises.

This hymn was an extract from the second section of a longer poem she had written on the life of Jesus entitled "The Old, Old Story". It was first published in 1866 with all royalties going to charity.

William Fischer was born in Baltimore, Maryland. He was a prolific composer of gospel hymns, music teacher at Girard College from 1858 to 1868, and then opened a piano store and music house in Philadelphia where he worked until his retirement in 1898. Fischer frequently led song services at revivals. He wrote the tune "Hankey" in 1869 and it appeared in "Joyful Songs" that year. Fischer also added the refrain to Hankey's verse. The completed hymn made it's first appearance in "Gospel Songs" by Philip Bliss in 1874, and in its present form appeared in 1875, in "Gospel Hymns and Sacred Songs" by Philip Bliss and Ira Sankey. The hymn became a favorite of the Moody and Sankey revival meetings.

Historical Setting For "I LOVE TO TELL THE STORY"

Alfred Nobel invented dynamite in 1866.
The underwater torpedo was invented in 1866.
The first postcards were introduced, in Austria, in 1869.
Mark Twain wrote "The Adventures of Tom Sawyer" in 1875.
The first roller-skating rink opened in 1875, in London.

I Love to Tell the Story

Words by ARABELLA K. HANKEY
Music by WILLIAM G. FISCHER

To God Be The Glory

Words by: Fanny J. Crosby (1820-1915)
Composed by: William Howard Doane (1832-1915) in 1875
Scripture Reference: Romans 15:6 Galatians 1:4-5

This hymn differs from most written by Fanny Crosby, in that it is more objective praise of God than subjective testimony or Christian experience. The exact year Crosby wrote this hymn text is uncertain, but it was probably in 1875, as she had the extraordinary ability to write songs on short notice to meet publication deadlines.

William Doane was born in Preston, Connecticut. He was a Baptist hymnwriter and composer of more than 2,200 melodies. This hymn first appeared in a Sunday school collection "Brightest and Best" compiled by Doane and Robert Lowry in 1875.

Historical Setting For **"TO GOD BE THE GLORY"**

The first American made Christmas card appeared in Boston in 1875.
The first Harvard-Yale football game was held in 1875.
Hires Rootbeer had its beginnings in 1875.

To God Be The Glory

Words by FANNY J. CROSBY
Music by WILLIAM H. DOANE

To God be the glory, great things He hath done! So
per - fect re - demp - tion, the pur - chase of blood; To
things He hath taught us, great things He hath done, And

loved He the world that He gave us His son, Who yield - ed His
ev - 'ry be - liev - er, the prom - ise of God. The vil - est of -
great our re - joic - ing through Je - sus, the Son. But pur - er and

life an a - tone - ment for sin And o - pened the
fend - er who tru - ly be - lieves, That mo - ment from
high - er and great - er will be Our won - der, our

life - gate that all may go in. Praise the Lord! Praise the Lord! Let the
Je - sus a par - don re - ceives.
trans - port, when Je - sus we see.

earth hear His voice! Praise the Lord! Praise the Lord! Let the peo - ple re -

joice! O come to the Fa - ther through Je - sus, the Son, And

give Him the glo - ry; great things He hath done! O done!
Great

There Is A Green Hill Far Away

Words by: Cecil Frances Alexander (1823-1895) in 1847
Composed by: George Coles Stebbins (1846-1945) in 1878
Scripture Reference: John 19:17-18

Cecil Alexander was an Irish poet and hymnwriter. This hymn is one of the poems found in the several volumes of poetic verse that she published in the 1840's and 1850's. This particular poem was written in 1847 three years before she married Rev. William Alexander, when her maiden name was still Cecil Humphreys.

It first appeared in her "Hymns for Little Children" in 1848. Most of the 400 poems and hymns written by Mrs. Alexander were written with the spiritual instruction of children in mind. This hymn was also written for children, but after the tune by Stebbins was composed, the hymn was used extensively in the Moody & Sankey evangelistic campaigns, and became a favorite of adults as well as children.

George Stebbins was born in Orleans County, Ontario, Canada. In 1874, he moved to Chicago and became a music director. Stebbins began working for Dwight Moody in 1876, as a noted song leader, choir director, composer, and compiler of gospel song collections. He composed this tune titled "Meditation" in 1878.

Historical Setting For "THERE IS A GREEN HILL FAR AWAY"

Thomas Edison and Alexander Graham Bell were born in 1847.
Salt Lake City was founded by the Mormons in 1847.
Evaporated milk was invented in 1847.
David Hughes invented the microphone in 1878.
A.A. Pope manufactured the first bicycles in America in 1878.

There is a Green Hill Far Away

Words by CECIL F. ALEXANDER
Music by GEORGE C. STEBBINS

There is a green hill far a - way, With -
He died that we might be for - giv'n, He

out a ci - ty wall, Where the dear Lord was
died to make us good, That we might go at

cru - ci - fied, Who died to save us all._____ Oh,
last to heav'n, Saved by His pre - cious blood._____

dear - ly, dear - ly has He loved And

we must love Him, too;_____ And trust in His re -

deem - ing blood And try____ His works to do._____

True Hearted, Whole Hearted

Words by: Frances Ridley Havergal (1836-1879) in 1874
Composed by: George Coles Stebbins (1846-1945) in 1878
Scripture Reference: Hebrews 2:9   Ephesians 6:10   Psalm 9:1

Frances Havergal was born in Astley, England. She began writing verse for publication at the age of seven, and was an accomplished pianist and vocalist, as well as being proficient in seven languages. It is said that Havergal always lived her words before she wrote them.

This hymn text was written in 1874 and published four years later. She wrote more than sixty-five hymns and many of her hymns first appeared in single leaflets and on ornamental cards. George Stebbins, a prolific composer, who attained the age of 99, published this hymn in 1878.

Historical Setting For **"TRUE HEARTED, WHOLE HEARTED"**

New York politician, Boss Tweed, was convicted of fraud in 1874.
Texas gunman, John Wesley Hardin, killed Sheriff Charles Webb in 1874. Three years later he was sentenced to 25 years in prison for the murder.
The Edison Electric Light Company was founded in 1878.
The first Tiffany glass was manufactured in 1878.
Bat Masterson began his career as a western lawman in 1878.

True Hearted, Whole Hearted

Words by FRANCES R. HAVERGAL
Music by GEORGE C. STEBBINS

1. True - heart - ed, whole heart - ed, faith - ful and
2. True - heart - ed, whole heart - ed, full - est al -
3. True - heart - ed, whole heart - ed, Sav - ior all

loy - al, King of our lives, by Thy
le - giance Yield - ing hence - forth to our
glo - rious! Take Thy great pow - er and

grace we will be; Un - der the stand - ard ex -
glo - ri - ous King; Val - iant en - deav - or and
reign there a - lone, O - ver our wills and af -

alt - ed and roy - al, Stong in Thy
lov - ing o - be - dience, Free - ly and
fec - tions vic - to - rious, Free - ly sur -

strength we will bat - tle for Thee.
joy - ous - ly now would we bring.
ren - dered and whol - ly Thine own.

CHORUS

Peal_____ out the watch - word! si - lence it

Peal_____ out the watch - word! si - lence it

True Hearted, Whole Hearted

never! / never!
Song of our spir - its, re - / Song of our spir - its,

joic - ing and free; / re - joic - ing and free;
Peal out the watch - word! / Peal out the watch - word!

loy - al for - ev - er, / loy - al for - ev - er,
King of our / King of our

lives, by Thy grace we will be. / lives, by Thy grace we will be.

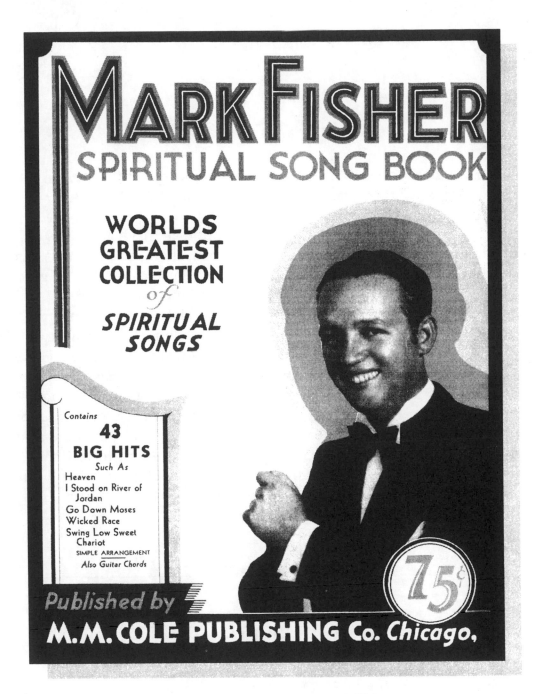

1933 Spiritual Song Book by Mark Fisher
Mark Fisher was called "The Golden Voiced Tenor"

Mark, just 5 years old was sitting in the kitchen of his home in Philadelphia listening to his mothers' cook sing spirituals and hyms while she was preparing supper. The first music he heard were these wonderful old time spirituals; many of which are contained in this book.

He studied to become an opera singer and organized his own orchestra in his late teens. After school he joined the famous Oriole orchestra and toured the country as the featured vocalist becoming an overnight sensation. He mastered the tenor banjo, formed his own orchestra and played at the Edgewater Beach Hotel in Chicago for many years. A noted composer of popular songs including "When You're Smiling" that is still a poplar song to this day. At the height of his popularity, in the 30s and 40s, he had several songbooks published but this was his only spiritual book.

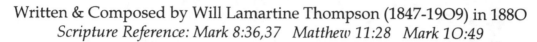

Softly And Tenderly

Written & Composed by Will Lamartine Thompson (1847-1909) in 1880
Scripture Reference: Mark 8:36,37   Matthew 11:28   Mark 10:49

Will Thompson was born in Beaver County, Pennsylvania. His father moved the family to East Liverpool, Ohio when Thompson was still a young boy. In college he majored in commerce and business and after graduation he opened a music shop in the back of his fathers general mercantile store.

Thompson began writing popular songs at age sixteen and then turned to hymn writing in later years. He enrolled in the New England Conservatory of Music in Boston, and in 1876 he went to the conservatory of music in Leipzig. He established the Will L. Thompson & Co. music publishing firm in his native East Liverpool, Ohio.

Thompson liked to carry a pocket notebook with him because he said, "No matter where I am, at home or hotel, at the store or in the car, if an idea or theme comes to me that I deem worthy of a song, I jot it down in verse, and as I do so the music simply comes to me naturally. So I write words and music enough to call back the whole theme again any time I open to it. In this way I never lose it." He wrote the tune "Thompson" for this hymn, for which he wrote both words and music in 1880. It first appeared in an 1880 collection "Sparkling Gems".

Historical Setting For **"SOFTLY AND TENDERLY"**

The game of Bingo was developed in 1880.
Lew Wallace wrote "Ben Hur" in 1880.
The Salvation Army was organized in the U.S. in 1880.

Soft and Tenderly

Words and Music by
WILL L. THOMPSON

Bringing In The Sheaves

Words by: Knowles Shaw (1834-1879) in 1874
Composed by: George A. Minor (1845-1904) in 1880
Scripture Reference: Matthew 9:37-38, Matthew 13:30, Psalm 126:6

Knowles Shaw was a native of Butler County, Ohio. He learned to play the violin as a teenager and was very much in demand at community dances. Shaw converted to Christianity in his teens and joined the Big Flatrock Christian Church across the road from the farm where he lived. He entered the seminary at the age of 19 and went on to be an evangelist for more than 25 years.

Shaw composed 110 songs and published five collections of songs between 1868 and 1877. He wrote both the words and music for this hymn in 1874, and he based the text of this hymn on Psalm 126 and Matthew 13:30. Shaw was killed in a railroad derailment accident near McKinney, Texas in the summer of 1879.

George Minor was born in Richmond, Virginia. He was a Baptist sacred music publisher, and wrote a new tune called "Harvest" for this hymn in 1880 which soon became more popular than the original tune by Shaw. Minor was a Confederate veteran of the Civil War.

This hymn has been one of the most popular revival meeting songs over the years.

Historical Setting For **"BRINGING IN THE SHEAVES"**

The song "O Little Town Of Bethlehem" was first published in 1874.
There were more than 100 millionaires in the United States for the first time in 1880.

Bringing in the Sheaves

Words by KNOWLES SHAW
Music by GEORGE A. MINOR

1. Sow - ing in the morn - ing, sow - ing seeds of kind - ness,

Sow - ing in the noon - tide and the dew - y eve; Wait - ing for the har - vest,

and the time of reap - ing, We shall come re - joic - ing,

bring - ing in the sheaves. Bring - ing in the sheaves, bring - ing in the sheaves,

We shall come re - joic - ing bring - ing in the sheaves. bring - ing in the sheaves.

2. Sowing in the sunshine, sowing in the shadows,
   Fearing neither clouds nor winter's chilling breeze;
   By and by the harvest, and the labor ended,
   We shall come rejoicing, bringing in the sheaves.

3. Going forth with weeping, sowing for the Master,
   Tho' the loss sustained our spirit often grieves;
   When our weeping's over, He will bid us welcome,
   We shall come rejoicing, bringing in the sheaves.

'Tis So Sweet To Trust In Jesus

Words by Louisa M.R. Stead (1850-1917) in 1880
Composed by: William James Kirkpatrick (1838-1921) in 1882
Scripture Reference: Ephesians 1:12
Psalms 22:4-5

Louisa Stead was born in Dover, England, and arrived in America in 1871. She married in 1875 and wrote this song during the days that followed the tragic drowning of her husband in 1880, while he was trying to rescue their four year old daughter, Lily, in the waters off Long Island, NY. Soon after this, Louisa left for missionary work in South Africa, where she served for 25 years.

William Kirkpatrick was from Duncannon, Pennsylvania. He was a Methodist music composer and wrote the tune "Trust in Jesus" for this hymn. A Union veteran of the American Civil War, he was in the furniture business from 1862 to 1878. He did much to promote the cause of early gospel music by editing and compiling hymns from 1858 to the end of his busy life. It is said that he compiled 100 gospel song books. This hymn first appeared in the collection "Songs of Triumph" in 1882.

Historical Setting For **"TIS SO SWEET TO TRUST IN JESUS"**

John Philip Sousa was appointed leader of the U.S. Marine Band in 1880.
The U.S. population topped 50 million for the first time in 1880.
Henry Wadsworth Longfellow, Ralph Waldo Emerson, and Jesse James died in 1882.
The electric iron was invented in 1882.

'Tis so Sweet to Trust in Jesus

Words by LOUISA M.R. STEAD
Music by WILLIAM J. KIRKPATRICK

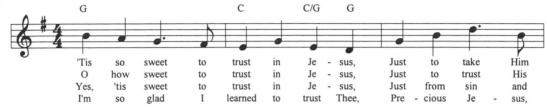

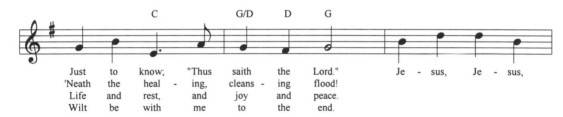

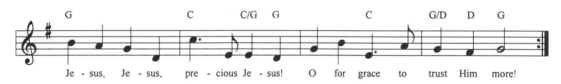

'Tis so sweet to trust in Je - sus, Just to take Him at His word,
O how sweet to trust in Je - sus, Just to trust His cleans - ing blood,
Yes, 'tis sweet to trust in Je - sus, Just from sin and self to cease,
I'm so glad I learned to trust Thee, Pre - cious Je - sus, Sav - ior, Friend;

Just to rest up - on His prom - ise, Just to know; "Thus saith the Lord."
Just in sim - ple faith to plunge me 'Neath the heal - ing, cleans - ing flood!
Just from Je - sus sim - ply tak - ing Life and rest, and joy and peace.
And I know that Thou art with me, Wilt be with me to the end.

Je - sus, Je - sus, how I trust Him! How I've proved Him o'er and o'er!
Je - sus, Je - sus, pre - cious Je - sus! O for grace to trust Him more!

135

God Be With You

Words by: Jeremiah Eames Rankin (1828-1904) in 1882
Composed by: William Gould Tomer (1833-1896) in 1882
Scripture Reference: Romans 16:20 Matthew 28:20

Dr. Jeremiah Rankin was born in Thornton, New Hampshire, and became a Congregational minister in 1855. In 1889, he became the president of Howard University in Washington D.C.

Rankin compiled a number of Gospel songbooks and wrote several hymns. He wrote this hymn text in 1882 and it was first sung at the "First Congregational Church" in Washington where Rankin was the pastor for 15 years. This popular benediction hymn has probably closed more religious services during the past century than any other hymn.

William Tomer served in the Civil War for the Union Army, was a government employee in Washington D.C. for 20 years, then became a public school teacher. He was serving as a music director at a Methodist Episcopal Church when he composed the tune "Farewell" for this hymn in 1882. The hymn was widely used in the Moody and Sankey revival meetings. It was first published in "Gospel Bells" in 1883.

Historical Setting For "GOD BE WITH YOU"

The American Baseball Association was founded in 1882.
R.L. Stevenson wrote "Treasure Island" in 1882.
Tchaikovsky composed his "1812 Overture" in 1882.
The Orient Express made it's first run in 1883.
Buffalo Bill Cody organized his "Wild West Show" in 1883.

God Be with You

Words by JEREMIAH E. RANKIN
Music by WILLIAM G. TOMER

Standing On The Promises

Written & Composed by: Russell Kelso Carter (1849-1928) in 1886
Scripture Reference: Hebrews 10:23 2 Corinthians 1:20

R. Kelso Carter was born in Baltimore, Maryland. This hymn was written and published by Carter in "Promises of Perfect Love" in 1886 while he was serving as a professor in the Pennsylvania Military Academy.

Carter was a talented individual. In his lifetime he was an outstanding athlete as a student, became a Methodist minister in 1887, spent time as a sheep rancher and served as a professor of chemistry, natural science, civil engineering and mathematics. Also, he was a publisher of textbooks, an author of novels, and a practicing physician in Baltimore late in life.

In 1891 Carter helped compile the Christian and Missionary Alliance hymnal "Hymns of the Christian Life" in which he contributed sixty-eight original tunes and fifty-two poems.

Historical Setting For **"STANDING ON THE PROMISES"**

Atlanta pharmacist, John S. Pemberton, concocted the soft drink Coca-Cola in 1886. Grover Cleveland became the only U.S. President married in the White House, in 1886. The first issue of "The World Almanac" was published in 1886.

Standing on the Promises

Words and Music by
RUSSEL K. CARTER

Stand - ing on the pro - mi - ses of Christ my King, thro e - ter - nal a - ges let His

prais - es ring; Glo - ry in the high - est, I will shout and sing,

stand - ing on the pro - mi - ses of God. Stand - ing, stand - ing,

stand - ing on the pro - mi - ses of God my Sav - ior. Stand - ing,

stand - ing, I'm stand - ing on the pro - mi - ses of God.

2. Standing on the promises that cannot fail,
When the howling storms of doubt and fear assail,
By the living word of God I shall prevail,
Standing on the promises of God. CHORUS

3. Standing on the promises of Christ the Lord,
Bound to Him eternally by love's strong cord,
Overcoming daily with the Spirit's sword,
Standing on the promises of God. CHORUS

4. Standing on the promises I cannot fall,
Listening every moment to the Spirit's call,
Resting in my Saviour, as my all in all,
Standing on the promises of God. CHORUS

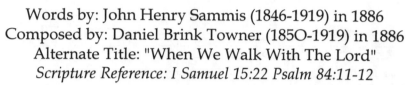

Trust And Obey

Words by: John Henry Sammis (1846-1919) in 1886
Composed by: Daniel Brink Towner (1850-1919) in 1886
Alternate Title: "When We Walk With The Lord"
Scripture Reference: I Samuel 15:22 Psalm 84:11-12

Daniel Towner suggested this song's title to the author, J.H. Sammis, after hearing a young man give his testimony at a Dwight L. Moody evangelism meeting, saying "I am not quite sure---but I am going to trust, and I am going to obey".

John Sammis was born in Brooklyn, New York. He became a Presbyterian minister in 1880, serving pastorates in the Midwest, and later became a teacher at the Moody Institute.

Sammis wrote the current five stanzas to this hymn, and the hymn made its first appearance in the collection "Hymns Old and New" in 1887. The hymn was also known as "When We Walk with the Lord". After Sammis wrote the words, Towner composed the music to it in 1886 and published the song in a collection of hymns in 1887.

Daniel Towner led the music for Moody evangelism meetings in the 1880's, then became director of the Moody Bible Institute of Chicago in 1893, where he remained until his death in 1919.

Historical Setting For **"TRUST AND OBEY"**

The last major Indian war in the United States ended in 1886 with the capture of Geronimo.
Avon Products & Sears, Roebuck had their beginnings in 1886.
Log Cabin Syrup & Ball-Mason jars were introduced in 1887.
The first Sherlock Holmes story was written in 1887.

Trust and Obey

Words by J. H. Sammis
Music by Daniel B. Towner

When we walk with the Lord in the light of His

Word What a glo - ry He sdheds on our way! While we

do His good will He a - bides with us

still, And with all who will trust and o - bey.

Chorus

Turst and o - bey, for there's no oth - er way To be

hap - py in Je - sus, But to trust and o - bey.

2. Not a shadow can rise, Not a cloud in the skies,
   But His smile quickly drives it away;
   Not a doubt nor a fear, Not a sigh nor a tear,
   Can abide while we trust and obey.

3. But we never can prove The delights of His love
   Until all on the altar we lay;
   For the favor He shows, And the joy He bestows,
   Are for them who will trust and obey.

4. Then in fellowship sweet We will sit at His feet,
   Or we'll walk by His side in the way;
   What He says we will do, Where He sends we will go,
   Never fear, only trust and obey.

Breathe On Me, Breath Of God

Words by: Edwin Hatch (1835-1889) in 1878
Composed by: Robert Jackson (1840-1914) in 1886
Scripture Reference: John 20:22

Edwin Hatch became an Anglican minister in the Church of England in 1859. Later he served as a professor of classical languages, and researcher of early church history, and ranks as one of England's most scholarly men.

He wrote this hymn in 1878 while he was vice-principal of St. Mary's Hall, one of the colleges of Oxford University. The hymn first appeared in 1878, in a pamphlet titled "Between Doubt and Prayer". The hymn text in its present form appeared in the "Psalmist Hymnal" in 1886.

Robert Jackson was born in Oldham, England. Educated at the Royal Academy of Music in London, he served as the organist at St. Peters Church in Oldham, from 1868 to 1914, a total of 46 years.

Jackson's father had served as the Oldham organist for the 47 years prior to 1868. Jackson composed the tune "Trentham" in 1886. It appeared in his "Fifty Sacred Leaflets" in 1888. The hymn is named after a small village in Staffordshire, England.

Historical Setting For **"BREATHE ON ME, BREATH OF GOD"**

Jehovah's Witnesses had its beginnings in 1878.
Calamity Jane gained notoriety for her heroic work as a nurse during the smallpox epidemic in Deadwood, Dakota Territory, in 1878.
The world's largest gold mines began operation in 1886 in Johannesburg, South Africa.
California shipped its first trainload of oranges to the Eastern U.S. in 1886.

Breathe on Me, Breath of God

Words by EDWIN HATCH
Music by ROBERT JACKSON

1. Breathe on me, Breath of God,
2. Breathe on me, Breath of God,
3. Breathe on me, Breath of God,
4. Breathe on me, Breath of God,

Fill me with life a-new,
Un-til my heart is pure,
Till I am whol-ly Thine,
So shall I nev-er die,

That I may love what Thou dost
Un-til with Thee I will one
Un-til this earth-ly part of
But live with Thee the per-fect

love, And do what Thou wouldst
will, To do and to en-
me Glows with Thy fire di-
life Of Thine e-ter-ni-

do.
dure.
vine.
ty. A - men.

Dear Lord And Father Of Mankind

Words by: John Greenleaf Whittier (1807-1892) in 1872
Composed by: Frederick Charles Maker (1844-1927) in 1887
Original Title: "Calmness in God Desired"
Scripture Reference: Isaiah 30:15

John Greenleaf Whittier is known as "America's beloved Quaker poet". He began life in Massachusetts as a farm boy and a village shoemaker, before entering the field of journalism in 1828.

From early on he admired the works of various poets, but his father felt that writing poetry was an unprofitable vocation, so he began editing newspapers in Boston and Philadelphia. Whittier was an ardent abolitionist and supported the anti-slavery movement. After the Civil War, he turned to writing more religious verse in his poetry and he became a poet of national stature by 1866.

These lyrics are taken from one of his major poems, "The Brewing of Soma", in 1872. It was first published for church use in Horder's "Congregational Hymns" of 1884. In this hymn, Whittier pays tribute to the self-knowledge that is found in solitude. He once stated that "a good hymn is the best use to which poetry can be directed", however, he never wrote a hymn intentionally. Editors selected verses from his writings to be used in hymns.

Frederick Maker composed the tune by the name "Rest" for this hymn in 1887. The tune was first published in London, in "The Church Hymnary", in 1887. Maker was an accomplished Irish musician, composer, music teacher and church organist who traveled extensively and lived in various parts of the world, but primarily in Bristol, England. It is said that he gave so many concerts in poor areas that he was known for accepting anything of value for his services.

Historical Setting For **"DEAR LORD AND FATHER OF MANKIND"**

Brooklyn Bridge was opened in 1872.
Yellowstone National Park was established in 1872.
The Statue of Liberty was dedicated in 1887.
The gramophone was patented in 1887.

Dear Lord and Father of Mankind

Words by JOHN G. WHITTIER
Music by FREDERICK C. MAKER

1. Dear Lord and Fa - ther of man - kind, for -

give our fool - ish ways; re - clothe us in our

right - ful mind; in pur - er lives thy ser - vice find, in

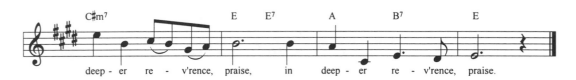

deep - er re - v'rence, praise, in deep - er re - v'rence, praise.

(The last line of each verse is sung twice)

2. In simple trust like theirs who heard,
   beside the Syrian sea,
   the gracious calling of the Lord,
   let us, like them, without a word
   rise up and follow thee.

3. O Sabbath rest by Galilee!
   O calm of hills above,
   where Jesus knelt to share with thee
   the silence of eternity,
   interpreted by love!

4. With that deep hush subduing all
   our words and works that drown
   the tender whisper of thy call,
   as noiseless let thy blessing fall
   as fell thy manna down.

5. Drop thy still dews of quietness,
   till all our strivings cease;
   take from our souls the strain and stress,
   and let our ordered lives confess
   the beauty of thy peace.

6. Breathe through the heats of our desire
   thy coolness and thy balm;
   let sense be dumb, let flesh retire;
   speak through the earthquake, wind, and fire,
   O still small voice of calm!

Leaning On The Everlasting Arms

Words by: Elisha Albright Hoffman (1839-1929) in 1887
Composed by Anthony Johnson Showalter (1858-1924) in 1887
Scripture Reference: Deuteronomy 33:27

Elisha Hoffman was born in Orwigsburg, Pennsylvania, and became a clergyman in 1868 in Evangelical, and later in, Presbyterian churches. He was a prolific writer of more than 2,000 Gospel songs, including this one in 1887.

Anthony Showalter was born in Chattanooga, Tennessee. He began teaching and publishing music at the age of twenty-two. He also became a Congregational minister.

Rev. Showalter not only composed the tune for this hymn in 1887, but supplied the words for the refrain. The scriptural text for the refrain is based on Deuteronomy 33:27. Showalter became a singing-school teacher in Hartsells, Alabama. He asked his friend and professional gospel song writer, Elisha Hoffman, to help complete the verses for this hymn. The hymn was then published in the 1887 "Glad Evangel for Revival, Camp and Evangelistic Meetings Hymnal".

Historical Setting For "LEANING ON THE EVERLASTING ARMS"

The Boone & Crockett Club to protect American wildlife from ruthless slaughter by hunters was organized in 1887 by a group which included Theodore Roosevelt. Congress made Yellowstone country a refuge for buffalo and other big game animals in 1887 at the persuasion of Theodore Roosevelt.

Leaning on Everlasting Arms

Words by ELISHA A. HOFFMAN
Music by ANTHONY J. SHOWALTER

What a fel-low-ship, what a joy di-vine, Lean-ing on the ev-er-
O, how sweet to walk in this pil-grim way, Lean-ing on the ev-er-
What have I to dread, what have I to fear, Lean-ing on the ev-er-

last-ing arms. What a bless-ed-ness, what a peace is mine,
last-ing arms. O, how bright the path grows from day to day,
last-ing arms. I have bless-ed peace with my Lord so near,

Lean-ing on the ev-er-last-ing arms. Lean - ing,

lean - ing, safe and se-cure from all a - larm.

Lean-ing, lean-ing, Lean-ing on the ev-er-last-ing arms.

More About Jesus

Words by: Eliza Edmunds Hewitt (1851-1920) n 1887
Composed by: John Robson Sweney 1837-1899) in 1887
Scripture Reference: Philippians 3:10,11 Chronicles 16:10

Eliza Hewitt was born in Philadelphia, Pennsylvania, and was an invalid for an extended period of her life due to a spinal condition. She was a Sunday school superintendent for many years in Philadelphia at the Northern Home for Friendless Children and the Calvin Presbyterian Church. Also, she was a prolific writer of children's poetry and Sunday school literature, and a close friend of Fanny Crosby.

Hewitt wrote this hymn text in 1887 and it was first published that year in a hymn collection called "Glad Hallelujahs".

John Sweney was one of the influential musicians and leaders of the early gospel song movement. He composed over 1,000 hymn tunes, and published more than 60 collections of sacred music. Sweney was born in West Chester, Pa., and became a professor of music at Pennsylvania Military Academy for 25 years. During the Civil War he directed the Third Delaware Regiment Band.

Historical Setting For "MORE ABOUT JESUS"

The Dawes Act bestowed U.S. citizenship on American Indians in 1887.
Legendary gunfighter, Doc Holliday, died in 1887.
Construction began on the Eiffel Tower in 1887.

More About Jesus

Words by ELIZA E. HEWITT
Music by JOHN R. SWENEY

When They Ring The Golden Bells

Written & Composed by: Dion de Marbelle (1818-1903) in 1887
Scripture Reference: Isaiah 25:5

Daniel A. (Dion) de Marbelle was born in France. He worked on a whaling ship in the early 1800's before coming to America and serving in the American Navy during the Mexican War in 1847.

After the war he toured America as a musician and actor with an opera company. Later, he became the very first clown with the Barnum & Bailey circus. Eventually he helped Buffalo Bill Cody organize the famous Wild West Shows.

His talents included being a ventriloquist, the ability to play almost any musical instrument, and he was an eloquent speechmaker.

He wrote and composed this song in 1887. The royalties he received for his songs were stolen from him and he died penniless.

Historical Setting For **"WHEN THEY RING THE GOLDEN BELLS"**

Popular song "Rock-a-bye Baby" was published in 1887.
The Inter-State Commerce Commission was created in 1887.
Pearl Harbor was leased by the U.S. from Hawaii for a naval station in 1887.

When They Ring the Golden Bells

by DION de MARBELLO

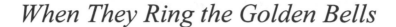

1. There's a land be - yond the riv - er That we
days shall know their num - ber, When in
know no sin or sor - row, In that

call the sweet for - ev - er, And we on - ly reach that shore by faith's de -
death we sweet - ly slum - ber, When the King com - mands the spir - it to be
ha - ven of to - mor - row, When our barque shall sail be - yond the crys - tal

cree; One by one we'll gain the por - tals, There to
free; Nev - er - more with an - guish la - den, We shall
sea; We shall on - ly know the bless - ing Of our

dwell with the im - mor - tals, When they ring the gold - en bells for you and
reach that love - ly E - den, When they ring the gold - en bells for you and
Fa - ther's sweet ca - ress - ing, When they ring the gold - en bells for you and

me. Don't you hear the bells now ring - ing? Don't you
me.
me.

hear the an - gels sing - ing? 'Tis the glo - ry hal - le - lu - jah Ju - bi - lee! In that

When They Ring the Golden Bells

far off sweet for - ev - er, Just be - yond the shin - ing riv - er, when they

ring the gold - en bells for you and me.   2. When our   me.
3. We shall

Hum _____

153

Take Time To Be Holy

Words by: William Dunn Longstaff (1822-1894) in 1874
Composed by: George Coles Stebbins (1846-1945) in 1890
Scripture Reference: I Peter 1:15,16 Leviticus 19:2 & 20:7

Wm. Longstaff was born in Sunderland, England. He was the son of a wealthy English ship owner, yet himself, was a humble and devout Christian layman. He was a close friend of Dwight Moody and Ira Sankey.

Longstaff wrote this hymn in 1874, after attending a Moody evangelistic meeting in Keswick, England, where he listened to a sermon on 1 Peter 1:16. and where he heard a story about Griffith John, missionary to China who had exhorted Christians to "take time to by holy." It inspired Longstaff to write this hymn poem which was to be the only famous hymn he ever wrote.

George Stebbins was an American Baptist music evangelist who was with the Moody organization for 25 years. He is credited with writing over 1,500 hymn tunes. His tune name for this hymn is "Holiness", published in 1890.

Historical Setting For **"TAKE TIME TO BE HOLY"**

Cartoonist, Thomas Nast, drew an elephant to represent the Republican Party in 1874. He had also drawn a donkey to symbolize the Democratic Party.

John Vincent founded Chautauqua, a system of popular education for Bible study and the training of Sunday-school teachers, in 1874.

Vincent Van Gogh died in 1890.

The Daughters of the American Revolution were founded in Washington in 1890.

Sitting Bull, chief of the Sioux Indians, was killed in 1890.

Take Time to be Holy

Words by WILLIAM D. LONGSTAFF
Music by GEORGE C. STEBBINS

1. Take time to be ho - ly, Speak oft with thy Lord; A - bide in Him al - ways, And feed on His word. Make friends of God's chil - dren; Help those who are weak; For - get - ting in noth - ing His bless - ing to seek.

2. Take time to be ho - ly, The world rush - es on; Spend much time in se - cret With Je - sus a - lone. By look - ing to Je - sus, Like Him thou shalt be; Thy friends in thy con - duct His like - ness shall see.

3. Take time to be ho - ly, Be kind in thy soul; Each thought and each mo - tive Be - neath His con - trol; Thus led by His Spir - it To foun - tains of love, Thou soon shalt be fit - ted For ser - vice a - bove.

When The Roll Is Called Up Yonder

Written & Composed by: James Milton Black (1856-1938) in 1893
Scripture Reference: I Thessalonians 4:15
Revelation 20:12

James Black was born at South Hill, New York. He became a teacher in singing schools, and edited more than a dozen Gospel songbooks.

While serving as a Sunday school teacher in Williamsport, Pennsylvania, in 1893, Black was taking a shortcut through a little-used alley and encountered a shy, raggedly dressed girl by the name of Bessie. He invited her to come to the class, which she did on that Sunday, but the following week when Black called the roll of the class she was not there.

Something in the experience of meeting the girl inspired him to write this song from start to finish in fifteen minutes and Black declared "I dared not change a note or a word". This song made its first appearance in his book "Songs of the Soul" in 1894. This collection of songs sold over 400,000 copies within two years of publication. This song is seldom found in hymnals, but is one of the best known of all gospel songs.

Historical Setting For "WHEN THE ROLL IS CALLED UP YONDER"

Henry Ford and Karl Benz individually made their first cars in 1893.
Cole Porter, American songwriter, was born in 1893.
The Flagstaff Observatory was erected in Arizona in 1894.
Victor Herbert composed and produced the first of his many successful operettas, Prince Ananias, in 1894.

When the Roll is Called up Yonder

Words and Music by
JAMES M. BLACK

When the trum-pet of the Lord shall sound and time shall be no more. And the
bright and cloud-less morn-ing when the dead in Christ shall rise, And the
la - bor for the Mas - ter from the dawn till set - ing sun; Let us

morn - ing breaks, e - ter - nal, bright and fair; When the saved of earth shall gath - er o - ver
Glo - ry of His res - ur - rec - tion share; When His cho - sen ones shall gath - er to their
talk of all His won - drous love and care. Then when all of life is o - ver and our

on the oth - er shore, And the roll is called up yon - der, I'll be there. When the
home be - yond the skies, And the roll is called up yon - der, I'll be there.
work on earth is done, And the roll is called up yon - der, I'll be there.

roll_____ is called up yon - der, When the roll_____ is called up

yon - der, When the roll_____ is called up yon - der, When the

roll is called up yon - der, I'll be there.   On that
Let us there.

God of Our Fathers

Words by: Daniel Crane Roberts (1841-1907) in 1876
Composed by: George William Warren (1828-1902) in 1894
Scripture Reference: 2 Chronicles 7:14

Daniel Roberts was born in Long Island, New York. He served as a private with the 84th Ohio Volunteers during the Civil War. He was ordained a deacon in 1865 and a Protestant Episcopal church clergyman the following year.

Roberts became vicar of St. Paul's Church in Concord, New Hampshire, and served there almost thirty years. Roberts wrote "God Of Our Fathers" in 1876, while serving as rector of a small Episcopal church, St. Thomas, in Brandon, Vermont. He felt the country should have a new national hymn for the occasion of the nation's 100th anniversary. His hymn was selected as the official hymn for the National Centennial Observance and is Roberts one claim to literary fame. For the centennial in 1876 his song was sung to the hymn tune "Russian Hymn". In 1889, the hymn was chosen for use during the centennial celebration of the United States Constitution.

George Warren had written a new tune to be used with this hymn at the 1889 celebration. Warren was an accomplished organist, and served in that capacity at Episcopal churches in Albany, Brooklyn, and then in New York City beginning in 1860. He was the organist at St. Thomas's Church for twenty years. The tune, National Hymn, Warren wrote for this song was first published in 1894, and it appeared that year in the "Hymnal for the Episcopal Church".

Historical Setting For "GOD OF OUR FATHERS"

During the Centennial year of 1876, Colorado became the 38th State.
Mark Twain published his novel "The Adventures of Tom Sawyer" in 1876.
George Armstrong Custer along with 265 men of the Seventh Calvary were killed at the battle of the Little Big Horn in June of 1876.
The Oklahoma land rush began at noon on April 22, 1889.
The Wall Street Journal began publication in 1889.
The U.S. Congress proclaimed "Labor Day" a national holiday in 1894.

God of Our Fathers

Words by DANIEL C. ROBERTS
Music by GEORGE W. WARREN

God of our fa - thers, whose al - might - y
Thy love di - vine hath led us in the

hand Leads forth in beau - ty
past; In this free land by

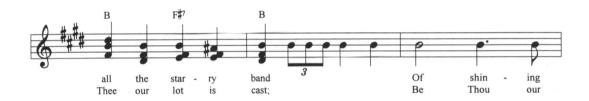

all the star - ry band Of shin - ing
Thee our lot is cast; Be Thou our

worlds in splen - dor through the skies,
Rul - er, Guard - ian, Guide, and Stay,

Our grate - ful songs be - fore Thy throne a - rise.
Thy word our law, Thy paths our chos - en way.

We Gather Together

Author Unknown
English Words by: Theodore Baker (1851-1934) in 1894
Arranged by: Edward Kremser (1838-1914) in 1877
Original Title: "Thanksgiving Prayer"
Scripture Reference: Colossians 4:2 John 11:52

Thanksgiving Day church services would not be complete without the singing of this traditional Dutch hymn. The original text was written in 1597 by an unknown author and published in 1626 by the Dutch composer Adrianus Valerius, and it was titled the "Thanksgiving Prayer". This was the same year that Peter Minuit and the Dutch were purchasing Manhattan Island in America from the Indians.

This hymn was used by the people of Holland to celebrate the Dutch freedom from Spain. The first Dutch settlers in America brought the hymn with them, and it eventually became America's favorite Thanksgiving Day hymn.

Theodore Baker served as the literary editor for G. Shirmer, Inc. from 1892 to 1926. He was a respected music researcher, and his "Biographical Dictionary of Musicians" in 1900, became an authoritative reference book for all serious music students. Baker translated this hymn into English in 1894.

Edward Kremser was born in Vienna, Austria. He became a choral director, composer, and publisher. Kremser found the text in 1877, and published it in a collection of his works. The tune name is titled "Kremser".

Historical Setting For "WE GATHER TOGETHER"

Peter Minuit purchased Manhattan Island from Indians in 1626.
The first Wimbledon Tennis championship was held in 1877.
Hershey Chocolate Company was founded in 1894.

We Gather Together

Traditional Dutch hymn
English words by THEODORE BAKER

1. We gath - er to - geth - er to ask the Lord's

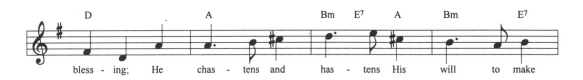

bless - ing; He chas - tens and has - tens His will to make

known; The wick - ed op - press - ing now cease____ from dis -

tress - ing, Sing prais - es to His Name;____ He for - gets not His own.

2. Beside us, to guide us, our God with us joining,
Ordaining, maintaining His kingdom divine;
So from the beginning the fight we were winning;
Thou, Lord, wast at our side, all glory be thine.

3. We all do extol Thee, Thou Leader triumphant,
And pray that Thou still our Defender wilt be;
Let Thy congregation escape tribulation;
Thy name be ever praised! O Lord, make us free!

Open My Eyes That I May See

Written & Composed by: Clara H. Fiske Scott (1841-1897) in 1895
Scripture Reference: Psalm 119:18

Clara Scott was born in Elk Grove, Illinois. She wrote the words and composed the tune "Scott" for this hymn in 1895. The inspiration for this hymn's title came from Psalm 119:18.

Mrs. Scott was a prolific composer of vocal and instrumental music. She taught music in the Ladies' Seminary at Lyons, Iowa beginning in 1859. She was married to Henry Clay Scott in 1861.

Scott was the first woman to publish a collection of anthems, in 1882. It was titled "The Royal Anthem Book". Clara Scott was killed in a carriage accident resulting from a runaway horse in Dubuque, Iowa, in June 1897. Her hymn first appeared in "Best Hymns No. 2" by Elisha Hoffman in 1895. It was published in the fall of 1897 in a collection of songs compiled by Scott titled "Truth in Song". Scott's untimely death kept her from knowing of the widespread popularity of her hymn.

Historical Setting For **"OPEN MY EYES THAT I MAY SEE"**

Automatic player-pianos began to be marketed in 1895.
The U.S. Post Office established rural free delivery in 1895.
The American Bowling Congress was organized in 1895.

Open My Eyes That I May See

Words and Music by
CLARA H. FISKE SCOTT

1. O - pen my eyes, that I may see
2. O - pen my eyes, that I may hear
3. O - pen my mouth, and let me bear

Glimps - es of truth Thou hast for me; Place in my hands the
Voic - es of truth Thou send - est clear; And while the wave - notes
Glad - ly the warm truth ev - ery - where; O - pen my heart, and

won - der - ful key That shall un - clasp, and set me free.
fall on my ear, Ev - ery - thing false will dis - ap - pear.
let me pre - pare Love with Thy chil - dren thus to share.

Si - lent - ly now I wait for Thee, Read - y, my God, Thy

will to see; O - pen my eyes, il - lu - mine me,
O - pen my eyes, il - lu - mine me,
O - pen my eyes, il - lu - mine me,

Spir - it di - vine!_____
Spir - it di - vine!_____
Spir - it di - vine!_____

We've A Story To Tell

Written & Composed by: Henry Ernest Nichol (1862-1928) in 1896
Scripture Reference: Revelation 15:4 Matthew 28:19-2O

Henry Nichol was born in Hull, England. He gave up a career in civil engineering to pursue the study of music. He earned his music degree from Oxford University in 1888.

He authored and composed this hymn in 1896, as well as several other sacred songs for special Sunday school services. This hymn was published in "The Sunday School Hymnary" collection of songs in the same year of 1896. For most of his songs he used his real name as the composer, but used a pseudonym, Colin Sterne, as the author of the words.

Historical Setting For **"WE'VE A STORY TO TELL"**

The first auto accident in the U.S. occurred in New York City in 1896.
The first Cracker Jacks and Tootsie Rolls were sold in 1896.

We've a Story to Tell

Words and Music by
HENRY E. NICHOL

1. We've a sto - ry to tell to the na - tions, That shall
2. We've a song to be sung to the na - tions, That shall
3. We've a mes - sage to give to the na - tions, That the
4. We've a Sav - ior to show to the na - tions, Who the

turn their hearts to the right; A sto - ry of truth and
lift their hearts to the Lord; A song that shall con - quer
Lord who reign - eth a - bove, Hath sent us His Son to
path of sor - row has trod, That all of the world's great

sweet - ness, A sto - ry of peace and light,_____ A
e - vil And shat - ter the spear and sword,_____ And
save us, And show us that God is Love,_____ And
peo - ple Might come to the truth of God,_____ Might

sto - ry of peace and light. For the dark - ness shall turn to
shat - ter the spear and sword.
show us that God is love.
come to the truth of God!

dawn - ing, And the dawn - ing to noon - day bright, And Christ's great king - dom shall

come on earth, The king - dom of love and light.

When The Saints Go Marching In

Written & Composed by: James Milton Black (1856-1938) in 1896
Scripture Reference: John 14:2,3

James Black was an active Methodist layman throughout his lifetime, and enjoyed being involved with the ministries of the Sunday school and youth work. Black moved to Williamsport, Pennsylvania around 1881 where he was an active member of the Pine Street Methodist Episcopal Church from 1904 until his death.

He was the only gospel song composer to serve on the joint commission for the 1905 "Methodist Hymnal". Black is credited with writing nearly 1,500 songs.

This lively hymn was written in 1896 and was popular with the jazz bands around the turn of the century. It was often used as a funeral march in the city of New Orleans. The tune became an important part of the musical score for a film, The Green Pastures, in 1936.

Historical Setting For **"WHEN THE SAINTS GO MARCHING IN"**

Helium and radioactivity were both discovered in 1896.
The first modern Olympics were held in Athens in 1896.
The Klondike gold rush began in Canada in 1896.

When the Saints go Marching in

Words by KATHERINE E. PURVIS
Music by JAMES M. BLACK

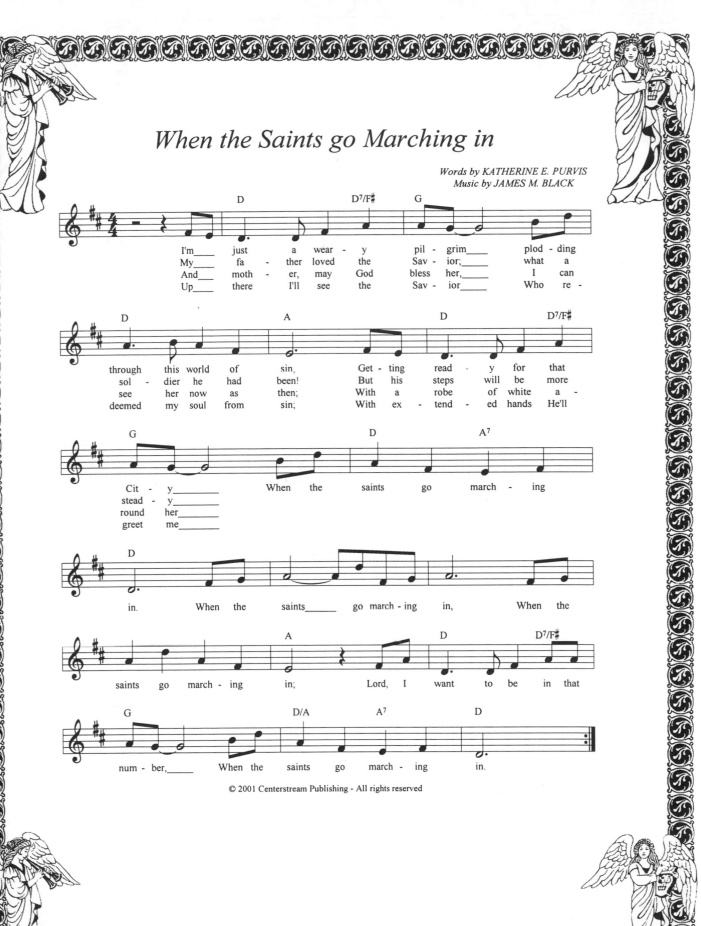

I'm____ just a wear - y pil - grim____ plod - ding
My____ fa - ther loved the Sav - ior;____ what a
And___ moth - er, may God bless her,____ I can
Up___ there I'll see the Sav - ior____ Who re -

through this world of sin, Get - ting read - y for that
sol - dier he had been! But his steps will be more
see her now as then; With a robe of white a -
deemed my soul from sin; With ex - tend - ed hands He'll

Cit - y_____
stead - y_____
round her_____
greet me_____

in. When the saints____ go march - ing in, When the

saints go march - ing in; Lord, I want to be in that

num - ber,_____ When the saints go march - ing in.

Count Your Blessings

Words by: Johnson Oatman Jr. (1856-1922) in 1897
Composed by: Edwin Othello Excell (1851-1921) in 1897
Original Title: "When Upon Life's Billows You Are Tempest-Tossed"
Scripture Reference: Ephesians 1:3 Proverbs 10:6

Johnson Oatman was born near Medford, New Jersey. At the age of eighteen he joined the Methodist Episcopal Church and then became a Methodist lay preacher. He preached at every opportunity, but worked in his father's mercantile business and eventually opened his own insurance office.

At age 36, he began writing religious poetry and became a prolific writer of gospel song poems. He is credited with over 5,000 hymn texts, many of which he sold for a dollar per poem. He wrote this hymn text in 1897.

Edwin Excell was born in Stark County, Ohio. Excell was converted at a Methodist revival, and turned his energies toward sacred music. He wrote both words and music to more than 2,000 Gospel songs, and published 50 Gospel songbooks.

This hymn first appeared in "Songs for Young People", compiled and published by Excell in 1897.

"Count Your Blessings" was also known as "When Upon Life's Billows You Are Tempest-Tossed".

Historical Setting For "COUNT YOUR BLESSINGS"

"There is a Santa Claus" was the response by the New York Sun to eight-year-old Virginia O'Hanlon in 1897. She had written a letter to the newspaper asking "Is there a Santa Claus?".

Jell-O and Grape Nuts were introduced in 1897.

Count Your Blessings

Words by JOHNSON OATMAN JR.
Music by EDWIN O. EXELL

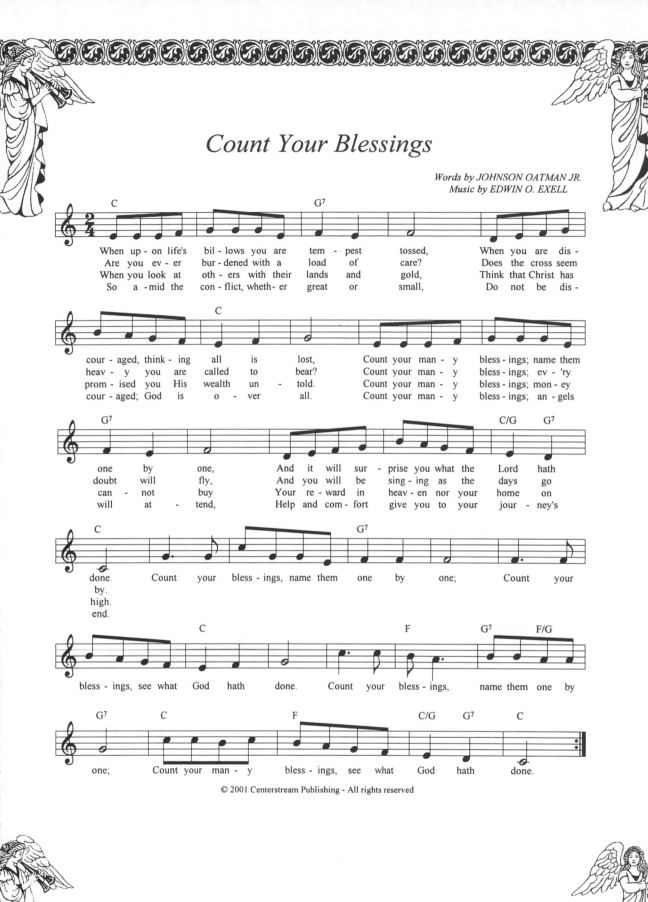

There Is Power In The Blood

Written & Composed by: Lewis Edgar Jones (1865-1936) in 1899
Scripture Reference: Ephesians 1:7,8 & 2:13 Revelation 7:14

Lewis Jones was born in Yates City, Illinois. He served as the director of the American Y.M.C.A. Hymnwriting was merely a sideline hobby and he was known to use three different pseudonymns. Jones graduated in the same class as Billy Sunday from the Moody Bible Institute.

This hymn was written at a camp meeting at Mountain Lake Park, Maryland and it was first published in the 1899 collection "Songs of Praise and Victory".

Historical Setting For **"THERE IS POWER IN THE BLOOD"**

Missouri first became known as the "show me" state in 1899.
The boll weevil crossed over the Rio Grande from Mexico to the U.S. in 1899 and began devastating Southern cotton fields.

There is Power in the Blood

Word and Music by
LEWIS E. JONES

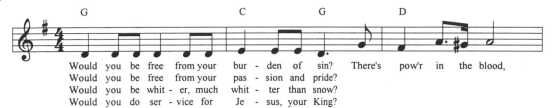

Would you be free from your bur – den of sin? There's pow'r in the blood,
Would you be free from your pas – sion and pride?
Would you be whit – er, much whit – ter than snow?
Would you do ser – vice for Je – sus, your King?

pow'r in the blood, Would you o'er e – vil a vic – to – ry win? There's
Come for a cleans – ing to Cal – va – ry's tide.
Sin – stains are lost in it's life – giv – ing flow.
Would you live dai – ly His prais – es to sing?

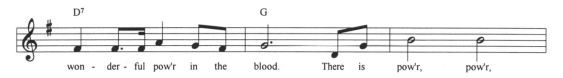

won – der – ful pow'r in the blood. There is pow'r, pow'r,

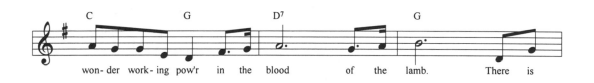

won – der work – ing pow'r in the blood of the lamb. There is

pow'r, pow'r, won – der – work – ing pow'r in the pre – cious blood of the lamb.

Just A Closer Walk With Thee

Author Unknown
Scripture Reference: Micah 6:8 2 Corinthians 13:4

Virtually nothing is known about the origin of this popular hymn. It appears to have gained popularity around the turn of the 20th century as one of the funeral marches played by New Orleans jazz bands.

Arrangements of this anonymous song have been credited to William Floyd, and Kenneth Morris.

Historical Setting For "JUST A CLOSER WALK WITH THEE"

The combined production of all U.S. automakers totaled about 400 cars at the turn of the century.

Women athletes began to take part in the Olympics in 1900.

The Indian population in the U.S. was down to an estimated 400,000 in 1900.

Just a Closer Walk with Thee

Traditional
Arranged by KENNETH MORRIS

I am weak but Thou art strong.　Je - sus, keep me from all
Thru this world of toil and snares,　If I fal - ter, Lord, who
When my fee - ble life is o'er,　Time for me will be no

wrong.＿＿＿＿　I'll be sat - is - fied as long＿＿＿＿ as I
cares?＿＿＿＿　Who with me my bur - den shares?＿＿＿＿ None but
more.＿＿＿＿　Guide me gen - tly, safe - ly o'er＿＿＿＿ to Thy

walk, let me walk close to Thee.　Just a clos - er walk with Thee,
Thee, dear＿ Lord, none but Thee.
king - dom＿ shore, to Thy shore.

Grant it, Je - sus, is my plea.＿＿＿＿　Dai - ly walk - ing close to

Thee,＿＿＿＿　Let it be, dear Lord, let it be.

God Will Take Care Of You

Words by: Civilla Durfee Martin (1869-1948) in 1904
Composed by: Walter Stillman Martin (1862-1935) in 1904
Alternate Title: "Be Not Dismayed Whate'er Betide"
Scripture Reference: Psalm 55:22

This hymn was written by Rev. Martin and his wife in 1904. The couple were in Lestershire, New York for a few weeks while Rev. Martin was teaching at Practical Bible Training School. During a brief illness, Civilla stayed at home one Sunday while her husband went to church. In the quietness of that day she was inspired to write a hymn about the assurance of God's care. Civilla showed the poem to Stillman when he returned home and he immediately sat down at a reed organ to compose the tune.

It was first published in the collection "Songs of Redemption and Praise" by John A. Davis in 1905. The hymn was also known as "Be Not Dismayed Whate'er Betide". This husband and wife team collaborated in authoring many Gospel songs. Civilla also wrote "His Eye Is On The Sparrow".

W. Stillman Martin was born at Rowley, Massachusetts and became a well-known Baptist minister. After a few years he joined the Christian Church (Disciples of Christ). In 1916 the Martins moved to Wilson, North Carolina, where he became professor of Bible at Atlantic Christian College. Three years later they moved to Atlanta, Georgia, and spent the following years conducting Bible conferences and evangelistic meetings throughout many states.

Historical Setting For "GOD WILL TAKE CARE OF YOU"

The Rolls-Royce Company was founded in 1904.
Cy Young pitched the first perfect baseball game in 1904.
The first neon light signs appeared in 1905.
Theodore Roosevelt began his second term as President in 1905.

God Will Take Care of You

Words by CIVILLA D. MARTIN
Music by W.STILLMAN MARTIN

Be not dis-mayed___ what e'er be-tide; God will take care of
Through days of toil___ when heart doth fail, God will take care of
All you may need___ He will pro-vide; God will take care of
No mat-ter what___ may be the test, God will take care of

you.___ Be-neath His wings___ of love a-bide;
you.___ When dan-gers fierce___ your path as-sail;
you.___ Noth-ing you ask___ will be de-nied;
you.___ Lean, wea-ry one,___ up-on His breast;

God will take care of you. God will take care of you,
God will take care of you.
God will take care of you.
God will take care of you.

Through ev-'ry day, o'er all the way. He will take

care___ of you; God will take care___ of you.

The Lord Bless You and Keep You

Composed by Peter Christian Lutkin (1858-1931)
Scripture Reference: Numbers 6:24-26

This is one of the most popular benediction hymns. The text is taken from Numbers 6:24-26. Peter Lutkin was born in Thompsonville, Wisconsin. He was a noted organist, choral conductor and lecturer on sacred music.

Dr. Lutkin was a founder of the American Guild of Organists in 1896. He taught at the Northwestern University School of Music from 1895 until 1931. He also served as an editor of early hymnals for both the Methodist and Episcopal Churches, in 1905 and 1918 respectively. This composition first appeared in the 1905 hymnal.

Historical Setting For **"THE LORD BLESS YOU AND KEEP YOU"**

Hiram Crouk, the last surviving soldier of the War of 1812, died in 1905 at the age of 105.

Will Rogers began his stage career in 1905.

The Carnegie Foundation was established in 1905.

The Lord Bless You and Keep You

PETER C. LUTKIN

Lord, I Want To Be A Christian

Author Unknown
Traditional Spiritual
Scripture Reference: 2 Peter 1:4   Luke 17:5

It is thought that the text for this song came from a remark by a Negro slave to a minister, William Davis, in the year 1756, "Sir, I want to be a Christian." The hymn was first published in the 1907 collection "Folksongs of the American Negro" by John and Frederick Work.

Historical Setting For **"LORD, I WANT TO BE A CHRISTIAN"**

1.29 million immigrants entered the United States in 1907.
The British Empire occupied 20 percent of the world's land surface in 1907.

Lord, I Want to be a Christian

Author unknown

Were You There

Author Unknown
Traditional Spiritual
Scripture Reference: Mark 15:25 John 19:18

Perhaps the most moving of all spirituals. The song was first published in "Old Plantation Hymns" in 1899, by William E. Barton, but it originated in the early to mid 1800's.

This hymn makes it clear to the listener that Christ's suffering, death, and ultimate resurrection must become a very emotional, personal experience and conviction in our lives.

The current arrangement first appeared in "Folk Songs of the American Negro" by John and Frederick Work, published in 1907.

Historical Setting For **"WERE YOU THERE"**

Coca-Cola was "bottled" for the first time in 1899.
The vacuum cleaner was invented in 1899.
The Ziegfeld Follies had their beginnings in 1907.
Maytag washers were introduced in 1907.

Were You There?

African-American Spiritual
Music by CHARLES WINFRED DOUGLAS

Have Thine Own Way Lord

Words by: Adelaide Addison Pollard (1862-1934) in 1902
Composed by: George Coles Stebbins (1846-1945) in 1907
Scripture Reference: Isaiah 64:8

Adelaide Pollard was born and reared in Iowa. She taught the art of public speaking in several schools throughout the northeast part of the United States. She worked as a missionary in South Africa, and Scotland during World War I.

Pollard was a very modest woman. She wrote many hymns, but did not sign her name to them. She devoted her life to the service of others. This hymn was inspired by the statement made at a prayer meeting, "Lord, it doesn't matter what you bring into our lives, just have you own way with us." Miss Pollard went home and wrote the hymn's stanzas that same evening in 1902.

George Stebbins composed over 1,500 Gospel song tunes. He worked with Ira Sankey in compiling several editions of the "Gospel Hymns" after joining the Moody organization in 1876. Stebbins published the composition for this hymn in 1907.

Historical Setting For **"HAVE THINE OWN WAY LORD"**

Caruso made his first phonograph recording in 1902.
The U.S. acquired control over the Panama Canal in 1902.
Conan Doyle wrote "The Hound of the Baskervilles" in 1902.
The first daily paper comic strip "Mr. Mutt" (later "Mutt and Jeff") began in 1907.
Harold Bell Wright wrote "The Shepherd of the Hills" in 1907.

Have Thine Own Way, Lord

Words by ADELAIDE A. POLLARD
Music by GEORGE C. STEBBINS

1. Have Thine own way, Lord! Have Thine own way! Thou art the Pot - ter; I am the clay. Mould me and make me After Thy will, While I am wait - ing, Yield - ed and still.

2. Have Thine own way, Lord! Have Thine own way! Search me and try me, Master, to - day! Whit - er than snow, Lord, Wash me just now, As in Thy pres - ence Hum - bly I bow.

3. Have Thine own way, Lord! Have Thine own way! Wound - ed and wea - ry, Help me, I pray! Pow - er all pow - er Sure - ly is Thine! Touch me and heal me, Sav - ior di - vine!

4. Have Thine own way, Lord! Have Thine own way! Hold o'er my be - ing Ab - so - lute sway! Fill with Thy Spir - it Till all shall see Christ on - ly, al - ways, Liv - ing in me!

Joyful, Joyful, We Adore Thee

Words by: Henry Jackson van Dyke (1852-1933) in 1907
Composed by: Ludwig van Beethoven (1770-1827) between 1817-23
Scripture Reference: Galatians 5:22   Psalm 71:23

Henry Jackson van Dyke insisted on this hymn being sung to Beethoven's "Hymn to Joy" from his Ninth Symphony. The combination of words and music makes this hymn one of the most joyous in the English language.

Van Dyke was born in Germantown, Pa. He loved nature and was an outstanding poet. After becoming a Presbyterian minister in 1879, and a professor of English in 1900, he wrote this hymn text while being a guest preacher at Williams College in 1907. He served as the Ambassador to Holland and Luxembourg for three years under President Wilson beginning in 1913.

The hymn text by van Dyke was joined with the hymn tune "Hymn to Joy" in 1911 and published in the "Presbyterian Hymnal" that year. Ludwig van Beethoven wrote his tune between 1817 and 1823, and it was first published in 1826.

Beethoven never wrote a tune specifically for a certain hymn text, but a number of his works have been adapted for hymns. The Ninth Symphony was Beethoven's last symphony, and is generally considered to be his greatest.

Historical Setting For "JOYFUL, JOYFUL, WE ADORE THEE"

Mississippi, Illinois, Alabama, Maine, and Missouri became States between 1817 and 1823.

Thomas Jefferson and John Adams both died on July 4th, 1826.

The 1st transcontinental airplane flight took place in 1911.

An early Mother's Day observance was held in Grafton, West Virginia in 1907 through the efforts of Anna Jarvis.

The first formal observances of Mother's Day were held the following year.

Joyful, Joyful, We Adore Thee

Words by HENRY J. VAN DYKE
Music by LUDWIG VAN BEETHOVEN

Joy - ful, joy - ful, we a - dore Thee, God of Glo - ry,

Lord of love, Hearts un - fold like flow'rs be - fore Thee,

Op'n - ing to the sun a - bove. Melt the clouds of

sin and sad - ness, Drive the dark of doubt a - way,

Giv - er of im - mort - al glad - ness, Fill us with the light of day.

I Would Be True

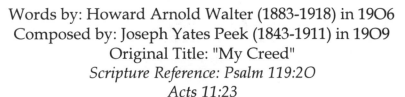

Words by: Howard Arnold Walter (1883-1918) in 1906
Composed by: Joseph Yates Peek (1843-1911) in 1909
Original Title: "My Creed"
Scripture Reference: Psalm 119:20
Acts 11:23

Howard Walter was born at New Britain, Connecticut. He wrote the first three stanzas of this hymn while teaching English at Waseda University in 1906. He sent his poem titled "My Creed" to his mother, who sent it to Harper's Magazine where it was published in 1907. In 1909, Walter showed his text to an itinerant, Methodist lay-preacher, Joseph Peek, who immediately began whistling a tune for the words.

Walter became an ordained minister, then joined the executive staff of the YMCA and went to India to teach Muslim students. He died in India during a severe influenza epidemic.

Joseph Peek was born at Schenectady, New York. He was a successful florist, and then became an itinerant Methodist preacher in 1904. Peek enlisted the help of a trained musician, Grant Colfax Tullar, in notating and harmonizing the music to "I Would Be True". His tune name for this hymn is "Peek", composed in 1909.

Historical Setting For "I WOULD BE TRUE"

The exact position of the magnetic North Pole was determined by explorer Roald Amundsen in 1906.
Greta Garbo was born in 1906.
The first "Ziegfeld Follies" was staged in New York in 1907.
Oklahoma became a State in 1907.
D.W. Griffith featured Mary Pickford who became the first film star in the U.S. in 1909.
W.H. Taft became the 27th President of the U.S. in 1909.

I Would Be True

Words by HOWARD A. WALTER
Music by JOSEPH Y. PEEK

1. I would be true, for there are those who trust me; I would be pure, for there are those who care; I would be strong, for there is much to suffer; I would be brave, for there is much to dare, I would be brave, for there is much to dare.

2. I would be friend of all the foe, the friendless; I would be giving, and forget the gift; I would be humble, for I know my weakness; I would look up, and laugh, and love, and lift, I would look up, and laugh, and love, and lift.

In The Garden

Written & Composed by: C. Austin Miles (1868-1945) in 1912
Scripture Reference: John 20:18

Charles Austin Miles was educated as a pharmacist and worked in that field for several years. Later he decided that Gospel hymn writing was more rewarding and became editor and manager of the Hall-Mack Music Publishing firm in Philadelphia in 1898. He also served as an editor with the Rodeheaver Music Company, and as a music director in churches, camp meetings, and conventions.

In 1912, Miles was asked by a music publisher to write a hymn that would be "sympathetic in tone, breathing tenderness in every line; one that would bring hope to the hopeless, rest for the weary, and downy pillows to dying heads". Miles wrote the words and the music all in one March evening. The hymn was inspired by the account of Mary's meeting with Jesus found in the biblical scripture of John 20. Miles related that "I wrote as quickly as the words could be formed, the poem exactly as it has since appeared".

Historical Setting For **"IN THE GARDEN"**

The "S.S. Titanic" sank on its maiden voyage in 1912.
The term "vitamin" was first coined by a Polish chemist in 1912.
New Mexico and Arizona became the 47th and 48th States in 1912.
The term "airplane" replaced aeroplane in 1912.

In the Garden

Words and Music by
C. AUSTIN MILES

I come to the gar - den a - lone_____ while the
speaks and the sound of His voice_____ is so
stay in the gar - den with Him,_____ though the

dew is still on the ros - es. And the voice I hear fall - ing
sweet the birds stop their sing - ing. And the mel - o - dy that He
night a - round me be fall - ing. But He bids me go; thru the

on my ear, the Son of God dis - clos - es. And He
gave to me with - in my heart is ring - ing.
voice of woe, His voice to me is call - ing.

walks with me and He talks with me, and He tells me I am His

own._____ And the joy we share as we tar - ry there, none

oth - er has ev - er____ known._____ He

I'd

3. known.

The Old Rugged Cross

Written & Composed by: George Bennard (1873-1958) in 1913
Scripture Reference: I Peter 2:24 Galatians 6:14

George Bennard was born in Youngstown, Ohio. He dropped out of school and became a coal miner at the age of fifteen. In 1907 he became a traveling Methodist evangelist, preaching in every state except Utah and Louisiana.

Although he wrote more than 300 Gospel songs, he had no formal musical education. Within 30 years of its publication, more than twenty million copies of "The Old Rugged Cross" had been sold, more than any other musical composition, of any kind, up to that time.

Despite the hymn's popularity, it brought Bennard little income and only small recognition. He often said he preferred to be remembered as a minister of the Gospel rather than a composer. "Hymn writing is just a runner-up," he said. The theme of the song, and the melody, came to Bennard quickly, but it took a few months before the inspiration for the words came to him, in order to complete the hymn in 1913. The hymn was completed in the kitchen of his home in Albion, Michigan. It was first published in 1915.

Historical Setting For **"THE OLD RUGGED CROSS"**

Henry Ford introduced the assembly line process in 1913.
The first crossword puzzle in the U.S. appeared in the "New York World" in 1913.
The U.S. dominated 40 percent of the world industrial production in 1913.

The Old Rugged Cross

Words and Music by REV. GEORGE BENNARD

On a hill far a - way stood an old rug - ged cross, The
old rug - ged cross, so de - spised by the world, Has a
old rug - ged cross I will ev - er be true, It's

em - blem of suf - fring and shame._____ And I love that old cross, where the
won - drous at - trac - tion for me._____ For the dear Lamb of God left His
shame and re - proach glad - ly bear._____ Then He'll call me some - day to my

dear - est and best For a world of lost sin - ners was slain._____ So I'll
glo - ry a - bove To___ bear it to dark Cal - va - ry._____
home far a - way, Where His glo - ry for - ev - er I'll share._____

cher - ish the old rug - ed cross_____ Till my tro - phies at last I lay

down._____ I will cling to the old rug - ed cross,_____ And ex -

change it some day for a crown._____ Oh, that crown.
To, that

Brighten The Corner Where You Are

Words by Ina Duley Ogdon (1872-1964) in 1913
Composed by: Charles Hutchinson Gabriel (1856-1932) in 1913
Scripture Reference: Titus 2:14 Revelation 22:16

Ina Ogdon, of Toledo, Ohio, spent a good deal of her life seeing to the needs of her invalid father, even though she had aspired to do greater things with her life. Her song, written in 1913, has often been considered the most popular gospel song of the first half of the twentieth century. It was composed by her friend, Charles Gabriel, and it became the theme song for the evangelist, Homer Rodeheaver, first introduced in a crusade in Wilkes-Barre, Pennsylvania, in 1913. Teddy Roosevelt used it to begin each of his political rallies across the nation in 1916.

Charles Gabriel was born in Wilton, Iowa. Gabriel was one of the best known and most prolific gospel songwriters of the late 19th and early 20th centuries. His songs were used by Homer Rodeheaver in the Billy Sunday evangelistic campaigns between 1910 and 1920. Gabriel became the music editor for the Rodeheaver Publishing Co., and is credited with writing over 8,000 songs and texts. Gabriel composed this hymn's tune in 1913.

Historical Setting For **"BRIGHTEN THE CORNER WHERE YOU ARE"**

The Indian head nickel (buffalo nickel) went into circulation in 1913.
Ping-pong became a popular new indoor game in 1913.
The Woolworth building in New York was completed and became the tallest building in the world at the time in 1913.

Brighten the Corner Where You Are

Words and Music by INA DUDLEY OGDON and CHARLES H. GABRIEL

Do not wait un - til some deed of great - ness you may do, Do not
all your tal - ent you may sure - ly find a need, Here re -

wait to send your light a - far. To the man - y du - ties ev - er near you
flect the Bright and Morn - ing Star. E - ven from your hum - ble hand the bread of

now be true, Bright- en the cor - ner where you are.
life may feed,

Bright - en the cor - ner where you are! Bright - en the cor - ner

where you are! Some- one far from har - bor you may guide a - cross the bar,

Bright - en the cor - ner where you are. Here for where you are.

This Is My Father's World

Words by: Maltbie Davenport Babcock (1858-1901)
Arranged by: Franklin Lawrence Sheppard (1852-1930) in 1915
Scripture Reference: Psalm 33:5 Psalm 50:12

Maltbie Babcock was born in Syracuse, New York. He was considered an outstanding Presbyterian minister. He pastored three prominent churches in Maryland and New York state.

Babcock wrote a 16-verse poem "Thoughts for Everyday Living" that was published posthumously in 1901. It was later reduced to four verses, set to music, and became this famous hymn. It is thought that Babcock wrote the verses several years before 1901.

Franklin Sheppard was born in Philadelphia, Pennslvania, and maintained a lifelong interest in music. In 1875 he moved to Boston to take charge of the foundry for his father's stove and heater manufacturing company. Sheppard was a layman in Episcopal and later in Presbyterian churches. He wrote the tune "Terra Beata" for this hymn. He served on the editorial committee of the 1911 edition of the Presbyterian Hymnal. In 1915, he edited a Sunday-school songbook titled "Alleluia" which included this hymn.

Historical Setting For **"THIS IS MY FATHER'S WORLD"**

President William McKinley began his second term, but was shot on September 6 by an assassin and died on September 14, 1901.

Andrew Carnegie retired from business in 1901.

The Victor phonograph company introduced the "Victrola" record-playing machine in American public schools in 1915.

D.W. Griffith produced his silent movie classic "The Birth of a Nation" in 1915.

This is My Father's World

Words by MALTBIE D. BABCOCK

1. This is my Fa - ther's world, And to my lis - t'ning ears, All na - ture sings, and round me rings The mu - sic of the spheres. This is my Fa - ther's world, I rest me in the thought Of rocks and trees, of____ skies and seas, His hand the won - ders wroght.

2. is my Fa - ther's world, The birds their car - ols raise, The morn - ing light, and the lil - y white, De - clare their Ma - ker's praise. This is my Fa - ther's world, He shines in all that's fair; In the rus - tling grass I____ hear Him pass, He speaks to me ev - 'ry - where. This

3. is my Fa - ther's world, O let me ne'er for - get That though the wrong seems oft so strong, God is the Rul - er yet. This is my Fa - ther's world, The bat - tle is not done, Je - sus who died shall be sat - is - fied, And earth and heav'n be one. A - men.

Great Is Thy Faithfulness

Words by: Thomas Obediah Chisholm (1866-1960)
Composed by: William Marion Runyan (1870-1957) in 1923
Scripture Reference: Lamentations 3:22,23

T O. Chisholm was born in Franklin, Kentucky. He became a schoolteacher at the age of 16, and later, a Methodist minister in 1903. He wrote 1,200 poems and many were used as hymn texts. From 1909 to 1953, he was a life insurance salesman.

The exact year he wrote this hymn text is uncertain, but it was one of a number of poems that he sent to William Runyan in 1923.

William Runyan was born in Marion, New York. He became a Methodist clergyman in 1891 and held various pastorates in Kansas. He later quit preaching due to deafness.

Runyan composed the tune "Faithfulness" for this hymn in 1923 and it first appeared in "Songs of Salvation and Service" that same year. From 1925 to 1948, he was closely associated with the Moody Bible Institute and Hope Publishing Company.

Historical Setting For **"GREAT IS THY FAITHFULNESS"**

A.C. Nielsen Company's rating service for the broadcast media was founded in 1923. The New York Yankees won their first World Series in 1923.

Great is Thy Faithfulness

Words by THOMAS O. CHISHOLM
Music by WILLIAM M. RUNYAN

Great is Thy faith-ful-ness, O God, my Fa-ther; There is no
Sum-mer and win-ter, and spring-time and har-vest, Sun, moon and
Par-don for sin and a peace that en-dur-eth, Thy own dear

shad-ow of turn-ing with Thee. Thou chang-est not; Thy com-
stars in their cours-es a-bove, Join with all na-ture in
pres-ence to cheer and to guide, Strength for to-day and bright

pas-sions, they fail not. As Thou hast been, Thou for-ev-er wilt
man-i-fold wit-ness. To Thy great faith-ful-ness, mer-cy and
hope for to-mor-row, Bless-ings all mine with ten thou-sand be-

be. Great is Thy faith-ful-ness! Great is Thy faith-ful-ness!
love.
side!

Morn-ing by morn-ing new mer-cies I see; All I have need-ed Thy

hand hath pro-vid-ed. Great is Thy faith-ful-ness. Lord, un-to me!

Are Ye Able

Words by: Earl Bowman Marlatt (1892-1976) in 1925
Composed by: Harry Silvertone Mason (1881-1964) in 1924
Original Title: "Challenge"
Scripture Reference: Matthew 20:22

Earl Marlatt was born in Columbus, Indiana. He was a professor of religion, and taught at colleges from 1925 to 1957.
He wrote this text for a consecration service at the Boston University School of Religious Education in 1925, based on the biblical scripture of Matthew 20:22.

The hymn was originally titled "Challenge". The text was joined with a tune composed by Harry S. Mason in 1924.

Historical Setting For **"ARE YE ABLE"**

The Ford Motor Company produced its 10 millionth car in 1924.
Insecticides were used for the first time in 1924.
The first Winter Olympics were held in 1924.
The Charleston became a fashionable dance in 1925.
The Chrysler Corporation was founded in 1925.

Are Ye Able, Said the Master

Words by EARL BOWMAN MARLATT
Music by HARRY S. MASON

1. "Are ye a - ble," said the Mas - ter, "To be cru - ci - fied with me?" "Yea," the stu - dy dream - ers an - swered, "To the death we fol - low Thee."
2. "Are ye a - ble," to re - mem - ber, When a thief lifts up his eyes, That His par - doned soul is wor - thy Of a place in Par - a - dise?
3. "Are ye a - ble," when the shad - ows Close a - round you with the sod, To be - lieve that spir - it tri - umps, To com - mend your soul to God?

REFRAIN

"Lord, we are a - ble," Our spir - its are Thine, Re - mold them, make us like Thee, di - vine. Thy guid - ing ra - diance a - bove us shall be bea - con to God, To love and loy - al - ty.

Love Lifted Me

Words by: James Rowe (1865-1933) in 1912
Composed by: Howard E. Smith (1863-1918) in 1912
Alternate Title: "I Was Sinking Deep In Sin"
Scripture Reference: John 3:14,15

James Rowe was born in Devonshire, England, and came to America in 1890. He devoted most of his life to writing songs and editing music journals. It is believed that he wrote over 19,000 song texts.

This hymn was a favorite with evangelist Billy Sunday. It was also known as "I Was Sinking Deep in Sin". Rowe and Smith wrote and composed the hymn in 1912 in Saugatuck, Connecticut.

Howard Smith composed the tune "Safety" for this hymn after Rowe had invited him over to his house to read the poem and work on a tune. With Smith at the piano and Rowe humming and singing a phrase at a time, the song took shape.

Smith was a long time church organist in Connecticut, but his hands were so crippled with arthritis that it was surprising he could play the piano or organ.

John T. Benson, Jr. composed a later popular tune for "Love Lifted Me".

Historical Setting For **"LOVE LIFTED ME"**

The first successful parachute jump was made in 1912.
F.W. Woolworth Company was founded in 1912.
Five million people in the U.S. visited cinemas daily in 1912.
Jim Thorpe won both the pentathlon and the decathlon at the 1912 Olympic Games.

Precious Lord, Take My Hand

Words by: Thomas Andrew Dorsey (1899-1993) in 1932
Composed by: George Nelson Allen (1812-1877)
Scripture Reference: Isaiah 41:13

This song was written from the broken heart of Thomas Dorsey in 1932, after the death of his wife and newborn son. Dorsey was a black gospel musician, who grew up in Georgia as a preachers "kid". He wrote over 250 gospel songs and adapted this hymn's text to a previously composed tune by George Allen. George Allen was born in Mansfield, Massachusetts. He was a music scholar and educator at Oberlin College in Ohio, from 1838 to 1864. Allen composed several hymn tunes, and laid the foundation for the Oberlin Conservatory of Music.

Historical Setting For **"PRECIOUS LORD, TAKE MY HAND"**

Frito corn chips, Skippy peanut butter, and 3 Musketeers candy bars were introduced in 1932.
The neutron was discovered, and the atom was split for the first time in 1932.

He Lives

Written & Composed by: Alfred Henry Ackley (1887-1960) in 1933
Scripture Reference: Matthew 28:6

Alfred Ackley was born in Spring Hill, Pennsylvania. He became a Presbyterian pastor in 1914, and a hymn composer along with his brother, Benton, for the Rodeheaver Publishing Co.

It is estimated that he wrote well over 1,000 gospel songs and hymns. This hymn was first published in "Triumphant Service Songs" in 1933.

Historical Setting For **"HE LIVES"**

President Roosevelt began his "fireside chats" over the radio in 1933.
The popular radio program "Lone Ranger" began in 1933.
The motion picture "King Kong" debuted in 1933.

Beyond The Sunset

Words by: Virgil P. Brock (1887-1978) in 1936
Composed by: Blanche Kerr Brock (1888-1958) in 1936
Scripture Reference: I Corinthians 13:12

This song was born during a conversation at the dinner table in 1936. A blind guest of the Brocks, Horace Burr, remarked how he could see "beyond the sunset". The simple phrase made an instant impact with Virgil and Blanche, and the hymn was completed before the end of the evening.

Virgil wrote more than 500 gospel songs, and worked together with Blanche in evangelism and hymnwriting.

Historical Setting For **"BEYOND THE SUNSET"**

Jesse Owens won four gold medals at the Olympics in 1936.
Hoover Dam on the Colorado River was completed in 1936.
The Baseball Hall of Fame was founded at Cooperstown in 1936.

How Great Thou Art

Original text by: Carl Boberg (1859-1940) in 1886
4th stanza by: Stuart Keene Hine in 1948
English translation by Stuart Keene Hine (1899-   )
Original Title: "O Store Gud"
Scripture Reference: Psalm 145:2,3

The original text was written by Swedish pastor, Carl Boberg, in 1886 and the song was sung to an old Swedish folk tune. A sudden summer thunderstorm inspired Boberg to write this poem titled "O Store Gud" (O Great God) which was later published in several periodicals.

The hymn was translated into German in 1907 by Manfred von Glehn and titled "Wie gross bist Du". An early translation into English was published in 1925 by Rev. Gustav Johnson in Chicago, under the title "O Mighty God", but it never caught on. In 1927, a 1912 Russian translation of the song by Ivan S. Prokhanoff came to the attention of Mr. and Mrs. Stuart K. Hine.

Rev. Hine and his wife were English missionaries to the Ukraine beginning in 1927 and they sang this song for many years in Russian. Mr. Hine translated three verses into English while they were in the Ukraine. When war broke out in 1939, it was necessary for them to return to England, where Stuart Hine wrote the fourth stanza of the hymn in 1948, which finalized the composition of this hymn as we know it today. The completed hymn was first printed in a Russian gospel magazine by Hine in 1949, and first introduced in America in 1951 when James Caldwell sang it at the Stony Brook Bible Conference on Long Island.

Historical Setting For "HOW GREAT THOU ART"

Robert L. Stevenson wrote "Dr. Jekyll and Mr. Hyde" in 1886.
Ty Cobb, American baseball player, was born in 1886.
Babe Ruth and Orville Wright died in 1948.
Israel was admitted to the UN in 1949.
Color television was first introduced in the U.S. in 1951.

How Great Thou Art

Words and Music by
STUART K. HINE

* Also "worlds"
** Also "rolling"

Author/Composer	Birth/Death	Place of Birth/Death
Alfred H. Ackley	1/21/1887 7/3/1960	Spring Hill, Pennsylvania Whittier, California
Sarah F. Adams	2/22/1805 8/14/1848	Harlow, Essex, England St. Martin-in-the-Fields, Middlesex, England
Cecil Alexander	1823 10/12/1895	Dublin, Ireland Londonderry, Northern Ireland
Chester G. Allen	1838 1878	
George N. Allen	9/7/1812 12/9/1877	Mansfield, Massachusetts Cincinnati, Ohio
Maltbie Babcock	8/3/1858 5/18/1901	Syracuse, New York Naples, Italy
Theodore Baker	6/3/1851 10/13/1934	New York, New York Dresden, Germany
Sabine Baring-Gould	1/28/1834 1/2/1924	Exeter, England Lew Trenchard, Devonshire, England
Joseph Barnby	8/12/1838 1/28/1896	York, England London, England
Ludwig van Beethoven	12/16/1770 3/26/1827	Bonn, Germany Vienna, Austria
George Bennard	2/4/1873 10/10/1958	Youngstown, Ohio Michigan
Sanford Bennett	6/21/1836 6/12/1898	Eden, New York Richmond, Indiana
James M. Black	8/19/1856 12/21/1938	South Hill, New York Williamsport, Pennsylvania
Philip Bliss	7/9/1838 12/29/1876	Clearfield County, PA. Ashtabula, Ohio
Carl Boberg	8/16/1859 1/7/1940	Monsteras, Sweden Kalmar, Sweden
Louis Bourgeois	c.1510 c.1561	Paris, France Paris, France
William Bradbury	10/6/1816 1/7/1868	York, Maine Montclair, New Jersey
Matthew Bridges	7/14/1800 10/6/1894	The Friar's Maldon, Essex, England Sidmouth, Devon, England
Blanche K. Brock	2/3/1888 1/3/1958	

Author/Composer	Birth/Death	Place of Birth/Death
Virgil P. Brock	1/6/1887 1978	Celina, Ohio Rives Junction, Michigan
Russell K. Carter	11/18/1849 8/23/1928	Baltimore, Maryland Catonsville, Maryland
Edward Caswall	7/15/1814 1/2/1878	Yateley, Hampshire, England Warwickshire, England
Thomas O. Chisholm	7/29/1866 2/29/1960	Franklin, Kentucky Ocean Grove, New Jersey
Elizabeth Clephane	6/18/1830 2/19/1869	Edinburgh, Scotland Bridgend House, near Melrose, Roxburghshire, Scotland
Charles Converse	10/7/1834 10/18/1918	Warren, Massachusetts Highwood, New Jersey
Fanny J. Crosby	3/24/1820 2/12/1915	Putnam County, New York Bridgeport, Connecticut
William Croft	12/10/1678 8/14/1727	Nether Ettington, Warwickshire, England London, England
Daniel de Marbelle	7/4/1818 12/18/1903	Seville, France Wayne, Illinois
Felice de Giardini	4/12/1716 12/17/1796	Turin, Piedmont, Italy Moscow, Russia
William Doane	2/3/1832 12/23/1915	Preston, Connecticut South Orange, New Jersey
Philip Dodderidge	6/26/1702 10/26/1751	London, England Lisbon, Portugal
Thomas A. Dorsey	7/1/1899 1/23/1993	
John B. Dykes	3/10/1823 1/22/1876	Kingston-upon-Hull, England Ticehurst, Sussex, England
Charlotte Elliott	3/18/1789 9/22/1871	Clapham, Surrey, England Brighton, E. Sussex, England
James Ellor	1819 9/27/1899	Droylsden, Lancashire, England Newburgh, New York
George J. Elvey	3/27/1816 12/9/1893	Canterbury, England Windlesham, Surrey, England
Edwin O. Excell	12/13/1851 6/10/1921	Stark County, Ohio Chicago, Illinois
Frederick Faber	6/28/1814 9/26/1863	Calverley vicarage, West Yorkshire, England Brompton, Kensington, Middlesex, England

Author/Composer	Birth/Death	Place of Birth/Death
John Fawcett	1/6/1740	Lidget Green, Yorshire, England
	7/25/1817	Hebden Bridge, Yorshire, England
William Fischer	10/14/1835	Baltimore, Maryland
	8/13/1912	Philadelphia, Pennsylvania
Charles H. Gabriel	8/18/1856	Wilton, Iowa
	9/15/1932	Los Angeles, California
Joseph Gilmore	4/29/1834	Boston, Massachusetts
	7/23/1918	Rochester, New York
Carl G. Glaser	5/4/1784	Weissenfels, Germany
	4/16/1829	Barmen, Germany
Henry Greatorex	12/24/1813	Derbyshire, England
	9/18/1858	Charleston, South Carolina
Arabella Hankey	1834	Clapham, Surrey, England
	5/9/1911	London, England
Thomas Hastings	10/15/1784	Washington, Connecticut
	5/15/1872	New York, New York
Edwin Hatch	9/4/1835	Derby, England
	11/10/1889	Oxford, England
Frances Havergal	12/14/1836	Astley, Worchestershire, England
	6/3/1879	Caswall Bay, near Swansea, Wales
Annie S. Hawks	5/28/1836	Hoosick, New York
	1/3/1918	Bennington, Vermont
Reginald Heber	4/21/1783	Malpas, Cheshire, England
	4/3/1826	Trichinopoly, India
Frederick Hedge	12/12/1805	Cambridge, Massachusetts
	8/21/1890	Cambridge, Massachusetts
Henri Hemy	11/12/1818	Newcastle-upon-Tyne, England
	6/10/1888	Hartlepool, Cleveland, England
Eliza Hewitt	6/28/1851	Philadelphia, Pennsylvania
	4/24/1920	Philadelphia, Pennsylvania
Stuart K. Hine	7/25/1899	London, England
Elisha Hoffman	5/7/1839	Orwigsburg, Pennsylvania
	11/25/1929	Chicago, Illinios
Oliver Holden	9/18/1765	Shirley, Massachusetts
	9/4/1844	Charlestown, Massachusetts
Robert Jackson	1840	Oldham, Lancashire, England
	7/12/1914	Oldham, Lancashire, England

Author/Composer	Birth/Death	Place of Birth/Death
Lewis E. Jones	2/8/1865 9/1/1936	Yates City, Illinois Santa Barbara, California
Thomas Ken	7/1637 3/19/1711	Little Berkhampstead, Hertfordshire, England Longbridge Deverill, Wiltshire, England
William Kirkpatrick	2/27/1838 9/20/1921	Duncannon, Pennsylvania Germantown, Pennsylvania
Phoebe Knapp	3/9/1839 7/10/1908	New York, New York Poland Springs, Maine
Conrad Kocher	12/16/1786 3/12/1872	Dietzingen, Wurtemberg, Germany Stuttgart, Germany
Edward Kremser	4/10/1838 11/27/1914	Vienna, Austria Vienna, Austria
William Longstaff	11/26/1822 4/2/1894	Sunderland, Durham, England Sunderland, Durham, England
Robert Lowry	3/12/1826 11/25/1899	Philadelphia, Pennsylvania Plainfield, New Jersey
Martin Luther	11/10/1483 2/18/1546	Eisleben, Saxony, Germany Eisleben, Saxony, Germany
Peter C. Lutkin	3/27/1858 12/27/1931	Thompsonville, Wisconsin Evanston, Illinois
Henry F. Lyte	6/1/1793 11/20/1847	Ednam, Scotland Nice, France
Frederick Maker	1844 1/1/1927	Bristol, England Bristol, England
Henry Malan	7/7/1787 5/18/1864	Geneva, Switzerland Vandoeuvres, Switzerland
Earl B. Marlatt	5/24/1892 6/13/1976	Columbus, Indiana Winchester, Indiana
Simeon B. Marsh	6/1/1798 7/14/1875	Sherburne, New York Sherburne, New York
Civilla D. Martin	8/26/1866 3/9/1948	Jordan, Nova Scotia, Canada Atlanta, Georgia
Walter S. Martin	1862 12/16/1935	Rowley, Massachusetts Atlanta, Georgia
Harry S. Mason	10/17/1881 11/15/1964	Gloversville, New York Torrington, Connecticut
Lowell Mason	1/8/1792 8/11/1872	Medfield, Massachusetts Orange, New Jersey

Author/Composer	Birth/Death	Place of Birth/Death
Christopher Meineke	5/1/1782 11/6/1850 3/10/1946	Oldenburg, Germany Baltimore, Maryland Philadelphia, Pennsylvania
George A. Minor	12/7/1845 1/29/1904	Richmond, Virginia
William Monk	3/16/1823 3/1/1889	London, England London, England
Edward Mote	1/21/1797 11/13/1874	London, England Horsham, Sussex, England
Hans G. Naegeli	5/26/1773 12/26/1836	Wetzikon, Switzerland Wetzikon, Switzerland
John Mason Neale	1/24/1818 8/6/1866	London, England East Grinstead, England
John H. Newman	2/21/1801 8/11/1890	London, England Edgbaston, Birmingham, England
John Newton	7/24/1725 12/21/1807	London, England London, England
Henry E. Nichol	12/10/1862 8/30/1926	Hull, Yorkshire, England Aldborough, Skirlaugh, Yorkshire, England
Johnson Oatman Jr.	4/21/1856 9/25/1922	Medford, New Jersey Norman, Oklahoma
Ina D. Ogdon	1872 1964	
Ray Palmer	11/12/1808 3/29/1887	Little Compton, Rhode Island Newark, New Jersey
Joseph Parry	5/21/1841 2/17/1903	Merthyr Tydfil, Wales Penarth, Wales
Joseph Y. Peek	2/27/1843 3/17/1911	Schenectady, New York Brooklyn, New York
Edward Perronet	1726 1/2/1792	Sundridge, Kent, England Canterbury, Kent, England
Folliott Pierpoint	10/7/1835 3/10/1917	Spa Villa, Bath, England Newport, Monmouthshire, England
William S. Pitts	8/18/1830 9/25/1918	Orleans County, New York Brooklyn, New York
Adelaide Pollard	11/27/1862 12/20/1934	Bloomfield, Iowa London, England

Author/Composer	Birth/Death	Place of Birth/Death
Elizabeth Prentiss	10/26/1818 8/13/1878	Portland, Maine Dorset, Vermont
Jeremiah Rankin	1/2/1828 11/28/1904	Thornton, New Hampshire Cleveland, Ohio
John P. Rees	1828 1900	
Edward F. Rimbault	6/13/1816 9/26/1876	London, England London, England
John Rippon	4/29/1751 12/17/1836	Tiverton, Devon, England Surrey, England
Daniel Roberts	11/5/1841 10/31/1907	Bridgehampton, Long Island, New York Concord, New Hampshire
James Rowe	1/1/1865 11/10/1933	Horrabridge, Devon, England Wells, Vermont
William Runyan	1/21/1870 7/29/1957	Marion, New York Pittsburgh, Kansas
John Sammis	7/6/1846 6/12/1919	Brooklyn, New York Los Angeles, California
Ira D. Sankey	8/28/1840 8/13/1908	Edinburg, Pennsylvania Brooklyn, New York
Clara H. Scott	12/3/1841 6/21/1897	Elk Grove, Illinois Dubuque, Iowa
Joseph Scriven	9/10/1819 8/10/1886	Seapatrick, County Down, Ireland Port Hope, Ontario, Candada
Knowles Shaw	10/13/1834 6/7/1878	Butler County, Ohio McKinney, Texas
Franklin Sheppard	8/7/1852 2/15/1930	Philadelphia, Pennsylvania Germantown, Pennsylvania
Anthony Showalter	5/1/1858 11/16/1924	Cherry Grove, Virginia Chattanooga, Tennessee
Howard E. Smith	7/16/1863 8/13/1918	 Norwalk, Connecticut
Horatio Spafford	10/20/1828 10/16/1888	North Troy, New York Jerusalem, Israel
Louisa Stead	1850 1/18/1917	Dover, England Penkridge, Zimbabwe
George C. Stebbins	2/26/1846 10/6/1945	East Carlton, New York Catskill, New York

Author/Composer	Birth/Death	Place of Birth/Death
Samuel J. Stone	4/25/1839 11/19/1900	Whitmore, Staffordshire, England Charterhouse, England
Arthur Sullivan	5/13/1842 11/22/1900	Bolwell Terrace, Lambeth, London, England
John R. Sweney	12/31/1837 4/10/1899	West Chester, Pennsylvania Chester, Pennsylvania
William B. Tappan	10/14/1794 6/18/1849	Beverly, Massachusetts West Needham, Massachusetts
Will L. Thompson	11/7/1847 9/20/1909	East Liverpool, Ohio New York, New York
Godfrey Thring	3/25/1823 9/13/1903	Alford, Somerset, England Shamley Green, Guilford, England
Dorothy A. Thrupp	6/20/1779 12/14/1847	Paddington, Middlesex, England St. Marylebone, Middlesex, England
William Tomer	10/5/1833 9/26/1896	Finesville, New Jersey Phillipsburg, New Jersey
Augustus Toplady	11/4/1740 8/11/1778	Farnham, Surrey, England Kensington, Middlesex, England
Daniel Towner	4/5/1850 10/3/1919	Towner Hill, Rome, PA Longwood, Missouri
Henry van Dyke	11/10/1852 4/10/1933	Germantown, Pennsylvania Avalon, Princeton, New Jersey
William Walford	1772 6/22/1850	Bath, Somersetshire, England Uxbridge, England
Howard A. Walter	8/19/1883 11/1/1918	New Britain, Connecticut Lahore, India
James G. Walton	1821 1905	
Anna B. Warner	8/31/1820 1/22/1915	Long Island, New York Highland Falls, New York
George W. Warren	8/17/1828 3/17/1902	Albany, New York New York, New York
Isaac Watts	7/17/1674 11/25/1748	Southampton, England Stoke Newington, England
Joseph P. Webster	3/22/1819 1/18/1875	Manchester, New York Elkhorn, Wisconsin
Charles Wesley	12/28/1707	Epworth, Lincolnshire, England

Author/Composer	Birth/Death	Place of Birth/Death
	3/29/1788	London, England
Samuel S. Wesley	8/14/1810	London, England
	4/19/1876	Gloucester, England
John G. Whittier	12/17/1807	Haverhill, Massachusetts
	9/7/1892	Hampton Falls, New Hampshire
Richard S. Willis	2/10/1819	Boston, Massachusetts
	5/7/1900	Detroit, Michigan
Samuel Wolcott	7/2/1813	South Windsor, Connecticut
	2/24/1886	Longmeadow, Massachusetts

reference

Christmas Music Companion Fact Book

by Dale V. Nobbman
Centerstream
Publishing

This fascinating book deserves a place of honor in every Christmas music collection! For 50 beloved traditional tunes, readers will learn the story of how the song came to be, the author and the historical setting, then be able to play a great arrangement of the song! Also includes: an essay on The Origin of Christmas Hymns and Carols; a Christmas music timeline and overview; Christmas music trivia questions & answers; the histories of six contemporary carols; an index of authors, arrangers, composers and translators; and much more! Songs examined include: Away in a Manger • Deck the Halls • Jingle Bells • Joy to the World • O Christmas Tree • O Holy Night • Silver Bells • We Wish You a Merry Christmas • What Child Is This? • and more!

00000272..$12.95

(1-57424-067-6)

Centerstream Publications
P.O. Box 17878, Anaheim, CA 92817
Phone/fax 714.779.9390 ~ email: centerstrm@aol.com
Web Site: centerstream-usa.com